Asian Arguments

ASIAN ARGUMENTS is a series of short books about Asia today. Aimed at the growing number of students and general readers who want to know more about the region, these books will highlight community involvement from the ground up in issues of the day usually discussed by authors in terms of top-down government policy. The aim is to better understand how ordinary Asian citizens are confronting problems such as the environment, democracy and their societies' development, either with or without government support. The books are scholarly but engaged, substantive as well as topical and written by authors with direct experience of their subject matter.

About the Authors

RUTH PEARSON is Professor of International Development at the University of Leeds, UK. She has undertaken research on women's work in the global economy, focusing recently on migrant workers and gendered globalisation, and has carried out empirical work in Latin America, including Mexico, Argentina, Bolivia and Cuba, as well as in Thailand and Europe. She has a particular interest in the intersections of women's productive and reproductive roles and their implications for understanding globalisation and crisis in the contemporary economy.

KYOKO KUSAKABE is Associate Professor of Gender and Development Studies in the School of Environment, Resources and Development at the Asian Institute of Technology, Thailand. Her research interests are centred on gendered mobility and migration in the Greater Mekong Subregion and the effect of regional economic integration on women's work and employment. She has undertaken empirical work in Thailand, Laos and Cambodia and has a special interest in women and transborder trade.

Thailand's Hidden Workforce

Burmese Migrant Women Factory Workers

RUTH PEARSON & KYOKO KUSAKABE

Zed Books

LONDON | NEW YORK

Thailand's Hidden Workforce:
Burmese Migrant Women Factory Workers
was first published in 2012 by
Zed Books Ltd, 7 Cynthia Street, London N1 9JF, UK and
Room 400, 175 Fifth Avenue, New York, NY 10010, USA

www.zedbooks.co.uk

FSC
www.fsc.org
MIX
Paper from
responsible sources
FSC® C013604

Designed and typeset in ITC Bodoni Twelve
by illuminati, Grosmont
Index by John Barker
Cover designed by www.thisistransmission.com
Printed and bound in Great Britain
by CPI Group (UK) Ltd, Croydon CR0 4YY

Distributed in the USA exclusively by Palgrave Macmillan, a division
of St Martin's Press, LLC, 175 Fifth Avenue, New York, NY 10010, USA

A catalogue record for this book is available from the British Library
Library of Congress Cataloging in Publication Data available

ISBN 978 1 84813 985 5 hb
ISBN 978 1 84813 984 8 pb

Contents

Acknowledgements

The authors would like to acknowledge the financial support of the International Development Research Centre (IDRC) Canada, and the personal encouragement of Dr Navsharan Singh of Regional Office for South Asia, IDRC. We also received excellent cooperation from Jackie Pollock and colleagues at the MAP Foundation in Thailand; as well as from Yaung Chi Oo Workers' Association Mae Sot and Bangkok Office; from Pattanarak Foundation, Sangklaburi district, Kanchanaburi province; and from a range of Burmese labour and other organisations, and international NGOs in Thailand.

We would like to express appreciation to our wonderful research team – Naw Eh Mwee, Lada Phadungkiati, Naw Htee Heh, Zin Mar Oo, Cecil Khin, Kanokporn Jaroenrith and San Sithilertprasit – for their tireless efforts in collecting data and translating documents and interviews. We also received research assistance from Krongwan Traitongyoo and Usamard Siampakdee. Thanks to Helene Dyrhauge for support with the manuscript and bibliography, and to Tamsine O'Riordan of Zed Books for her enthusiasm and guidance in preparing this book. We also pay tribute to all the migrant workers from Burma who shared their experiences with us and wish them well in this crucial moment in their country's history.

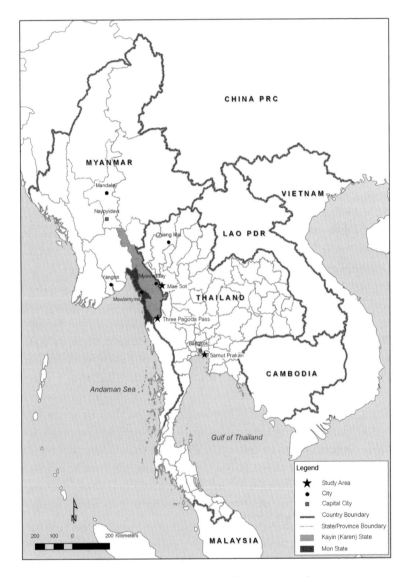

Thailand and surrounding countries

Abbreviations

ACMECS	Ayeyarwady–Chaophraya–Mekong Economic Cooperation Strategy
ASEAN	Association of Southeast Asian Nations
BEAN	Border Essan Action Network
BLSO	Burma Labour Solidarity Organization
BMWEC	Burmese Migrant Workers' Education Committee
CDC	Children's Development Centre
COMMIT	Coordinated Mekong Ministerial Initiative against Trafficking
CPPCR	Committee for the Promotion and Protection of Child Rights
DKBA	Democratic Karen Buddhist Army
ECS	Economic Cooperation Strategy
FTUB	Federation of Trade Unions – Burma
GMS	Greater Mekong Subregion
ILO	International Labour Organization
IOM	International Organization for Migration
ITUC	International Trade Union Confederation
KNU	Karen National Union
MOU	memorandum of understanding

NGO	non-governmental organisation
NICs	newly industrialised countries
NLD	National League for Democracy
NRIE	Northern Region Industrial Estate
SAW	Social Action for Women
SPDC	State Peace and Development Council
TGMA	Thai Garment Manufacturers' Association
3D	dirty, dangerous and demeaning
UNHCR	United Nations High Commissioner for Refugees
YCOWA	Yaung Chi Oo Workers' Association

I

Thailand's hidden workforce: Burmese women factory workers

Burmese migrant workers in Thailand: hidden from the global gaze

This book tells the story of women who migrate from Burma[1] to work, as part of a large and exploited workforce, in Thailand's export factories. It deals with a part of the current globalisation story which is rarely glimpsed either from the West or indeed within Thailand and other parts of Asia. Most of the migrant factory workers in Thailand, like factory workers in garment and textile industries all over the world, are young women, though there are also a number of older women and men among their number. Their experiences of exploitation echo those of many women workers in export factories all over the world.[2] But what is particularly poignant about the story of the Burmese workers in Thailand is that they are not only migrants, seeking better lives for themselves and their families, away from the dire situation they face in their native country;[3] very often they are illegal or 'unregistered' migrants, with no legal right to remain in the country of destination, or even in their jobs. They have no recourse to legal protection from any kind of oppression or abuse, be it low wages, excessive overtime, harsh factory regimes, illegal deductions from their wages, restrictions on their mobility, or harassment by police, immigration authorities and local citizens. Although courted by Thai industrialists seeking to access cheap labour in order to make their products competitive in global markets often characterised as 'a race to the bottom',[4] Burmese migrants are frequently reviled by Thai people, who view them as a threat to social stability and job opportunities for themselves, a perception frequently fuelled by politicians seeking to distance themselves from the reality of domestic civil unrest and economic problems within Thailand.

There are an estimated 2 million migrant workers in Thailand,[5] most of whom work in the unregulated construction and agricultural sectors, moving between workplaces and employers as demand for their labour shifts, living in miserable conditions without regulation or protection. This represents a significant number given that the total recorded labour force in Thailand is some 11 million,[6] though there is very little acknowledgement, either within Thailand or outside, of the significant role played by migrant labour in the Thai economy. This contrasts strongly with the widely discussed presence of approximately 150,000 Burmese refugees who have sought shelter in a series of camps for displaced people on the Western borders with Burma,[7] which have received widespread publicity both in Thailand and throughout the Western world, particularly in North America, which is home to a relatively large Burmese diaspora.

The context: push-and-pull factors underlying Burmese migration to Thailand

The Burmese women and men who cross Thailand's border in search of employment conform in many ways to a classic model of push–pull migration. Certainly the economic and political conditions in their homeland provide a clear rationale for those who want to leave. Three decades of economic decline and political repression in Burma under increasingly oppressive military regimes have decimated the country's once substantial physical infrastructure and thriving economic sectors, which once supplied rubber to many parts of the world.[8] The ousting of Aung San Suu Kyi after her victory in the 1990 democratic general election heralded the rule of a series of autocratic and idiosyncratic military generals, often seemingly ruled by astrology rather than logic,[9] who have denied the population the opportunity for political participation or economic advancement. These governments have sought to impose the dominance of the ruling Burman ethnic groups against other ethnic groups, including the Karen, Karenni, Shan and Mon, who have at various times conducted armed insurrection against the government. This has not only resulted in the displacement of hundreds of thousands of people, but has also led to the development of a forced labour regime in which the government requisitions labour for the armed forces or construction projects, as well as food and other goods from minority populations. Repression is particularly strong in the border provinces, causing real hardship and insecurity as well as various types of human rights abuse.[10]

Even those from the central Burman heartlands have faced increasing economic insecurity as well as political oppression, and the migrant workers in Thailand come from all ethnic groups in the population. Most of the migrant workers we talked to recount tales of families falling into debt, with no possibility of jobs or incomes in the crumbling economy, claiming they are motivated to seek work in Thailand as much to support their families back home as to seek a better life for themselves. The push factors have been exacerbated in recent years by escalating repression and unrest. The so-called 'saffron revolution' in 2007 led by Buddhist monks on the streets of Yangon (Rangoon[11]), which was followed by severe repression of the students and ordinary citizens who gave their support to these protests. Those who came from the Irrawaddy Delta were further destabilised by Cyclone Nargis, which hit in 2008, with people in rural communities losing their homes as well as their land and livelihoods,[12] leading to further pressure on people to seek opportunities elsewhere.[13]

Indeed, working in Thailand does seem to offer a solution, particularly to their economic problems. The difference in wages between Thailand and Burma is large; official estimates say that wages in Thailand are up to ten times higher than in Burma,[14] which makes it very clear why young Burmese women and men are attracted to working in factories and in other parts of the Thai economy, in spite of difficult conditions and low wages in comparison to the pay of Thai workers. Many migrant workers we spoke to told us with pride that, although their wages were low, they were able to save money and send regular remittances to their families, whereas if they had stayed at home they would not have been able to help in this way. They also complained that in Burma the cost of education, transport and health was growing continuously, and wages at home, if they had jobs, would not cover all the family's expenses.

The growth of migrant workers in manufacturing and export factories in Burma dates from the 1990s, when Thai exports were increasingly challenged by competition from lower-waged economies in the region such as Vietnam and China. In order to take advantage of cheaper labour both in lower-wage parts of Thailand and in the form of migrants from neighbouring countries, the Thai government instituted a policy of industrial decentralisation, with the overt objective of closing the development gap between itself and its poorer neighbours. Whilst this objective has never been achieved, there has since the mid-1990s been a significant growth in factories employing migrant labour, and especially after the Asian financial crisis in 1997–98, which forced the pace of economic recovery measures. The majority of the factories (re)locating to border areas were set up in the western town of Mae Sot in Tak province. By 2004 there were nearly 125,000 registered Burmese workers in Tak province, though this is widely considered to represent less than a third of the total number of migrants, including those not official registered, making it the largest concentration of registered Burmese migrants outside Bangkok. The high proportion of women among these migrants – nearly

70 per cent – reflects the high concentration of employment in Tak province in garment and textile factories, which traditionally employ a high percentage of women in their workforce. Mae Sot grew from a small and isolated border trading outpost with 50,000 inhabitants in 1988, most notable for its (contraband) trade with neighbouring Burma in precious gemstones and teak, to a bustling urban centre ten years later with a resident population of traders – mainly Burmese Muslims and Chinese – supplemented by Buddhist Burman and Christian Karen workers from different parts of Burma. The population had grown fivefold by 2010.

Not all factories relocated to the border towns; still the largest concentration of Burmese and other migrant workers in Thailand are to be found in the small workshops and factories in central Thailand, both in the capital Bangkok and in other towns in the adjacent provinces of Pathumthani and Samut Prakan. More recently there has been a growth in the establishment of factories employing Burmese migrants in the town known as 'Three Pagodas Pass', a border crossing point in the Sangklaburi district of Kanchanaburi province; since 1996 a number have been producing garments, furniture and even mosquito nets, aimed at both domestic and export markets.[15] In this part of Thailand, unlike in the central areas and Mae Sot, the organisation of migrant workers is fairly informal due to the fact that this area is relatively isolated both from Yangon and from Bangkok, with poor road infrastructure on both sides of the border. Most of the Burmese workers employed in Three Pagodas Pass walk daily through the informal crossings that straddle the town, returning to their homes on the Burmese side when their shifts have ended; the exception is those – not infrequent – occasions when they are forced by the demands of the job to work all night, which requires them to sleep in the very place where they work all day.

The other concentration of Burmese workers, in the central provinces around Bangkok, are those who have been hit the hardest by economic downturn, first in the Asian financial crisis of the 1990s, and more recently in the deteriorating conditions of

2008–09, following the financial crisis in the West. The export factories only started to hire Burmese workers after the 1997–08 crisis as an alternative strategy to decentralisation, in order to reduce costs and improve their competitiveness. Many of the factories in these areas are relatively large, though they tend to coexist with informal workshops and home-based subcontracting. The larger factories generally employ only registered migrants who have the appropriate documents, often people who have been in the country for some time. Undocumented migrants can be found in the more informal workshops, where the pay and the working conditions are inferior.

Mae Sot and Three Pagodas Pass feel like migrant towns, delinked from mainstream Thai society, whereas the high numbers of (mainly) Burmese migrants in the town of Samut Prakan in central Thailand fail to make a significant impact on this large Thai city, except maybe in certain marginal neighbourhoods where migrant workers and their families are concentrated. Unlike in Mae Sot and Three Pagodas Pass, where migrants wear traditional Burmese dress (women in *salong* and men in *longi*), Burmese people in Samut Prakan tend to make more effort – and have more opportunities – to assimilate into Thai society. When they go out – even to the weekend language schools, which teach both Thai and English – migrant workers, in white shirts and black skirts, resemble Thai university students. Their clothing, like their tendency to display photographs of the Thai royal family, is a deliberate attempt to demonstrate 'respect' to the local Thai population. However, in Mae Sot, where only 5 per cent of the registered workforce in the garment factories are Thai, there is very little pressure to imitate the dress or other lifestyle preferences of Thai people

Background to the research

This book is based on research carried out by the authors, together with a team of Thai and Burmese researchers, between 2006 and

2010. The studies, focused on the three areas described above, involved interviews, surveys and participatory workshops with large numbers of Burmese workers and organisations, as well as Thai officials, policymakers and other key informants, including academics and international bodies.[16] In the course of this investigation we uncovered a great deal of information about the ways in which this hidden workforce, mainly young women,[17] is contributing to the economic development of Thailand, as well as working to support themselves and their families. We came to understand the complexities of the changing migrant registration system in Thailand, and the ways in which it serves both to discipline and to control the workers, and to provide a cover for a much larger number of unregistered – and more vulnerable – migrants. We became aware of the ways in which many Burmese migrant women live their lives without the recognition or protection provided by citizenship in either their state of origin, Burma, or their state of destination, Thailand, which is not the case for many migrant workers in other parts of the world, nor indeed for Thai migrant workers in other parts of Asia and elsewhere.

As noted above, the majority of this migrant workforce employed in Thailand's factories are women, mainly young women of prime reproductive age. One of the most striking findings of this study was the problems that arise when these young women have children. In the hostile environment in which they find themselves, they have to make complicated and difficult arrangements to access the maternity care they need for their pregnancy and childbirth, as well as securing the means for the upkeep and care of their children. Whilst the literature has reflected extensive concern regarding the so-called global care chain[18] – involving women from low-income developing countries migrating to developed countries to carry out care work in households, childcare centres, hospitals and care homes – there has been much less interest in the situation of other types of migrant workers and how they arrange their own care responsibilities, as they continue to carry out their jobs and provide economic support for their families.

The following sections of this introductory chapter provide an overview of the literature on and debates about migrant women in export factories. The chapters that follow report on the results of our research, providing detail of the context in which the growth of migrant women workers in Thailand has occurred. Our account focuses particularly on the journeys of the women themselves, the struggles they have undertaken to balance the different demands on them, the ways in which they have responded to their new circumstances, and the hopes and fears they have for the future and that of their families and children.

Burmese women workers in Thailand: nimble fingers and docile bodies

The Burmese migrant workers in Thailand featured in this book are part of a worldwide army of female workers who have laboured long and hard producing manufactured goods: both low-tech traditional products of the so-called 'sunset' industries, such as textiles, garments and shoes, and the new-wave products of the high-tech 'sunrise' industries, including home communications and media items (televisions, DVD players), computers, mobile phones, as well as the new generation of must-have consumer goods such as e-readers, iPads and the like. Since the 1970s, a combination of improved air and maritime transportation, telecommunications, rising costs and improved labour rights in the developed countries, as well as competition from the then emerging economies of the East – Japan and South Korea – encouraged corporations to seek lower wage platforms for the assembly and production of goods destined for Western consumer markets. Initially this was focused on the labour-intensive parts of a specific process – for example, the assembly of integrated circuits for the burgeoning electronics industries, the making up of garments from pre-cut cloth. In the first decade of this new international division of labour, such production was limited to the so-called 'Asian Tigers' – Hong Kong, Taiwan, Singapore and South Korea. But as the years went on more and more countries – the so-called newly industrialised countries (NICs), which included Mexico, Malaysia, Indonesia and Thailand – were participating in this growing market for manufactured exports. In the 1990s they were joined by even lower-waged economies: for example, Sri Lanka, Bangladesh and Vietnam in Asia; El Salvador, Nicaragua and Costa Rica in Central America; and Morocco, Egypt, Mauritius and Mauritania in North and sub-Saharan Africa. Production in some of the early global industrialisers became more integrated, more capital-intensive – and less female-intensive – whilst those at the lowest end of the supply chain, mainly working in low-tech garment and other assembly industries, competed increasingly on the basis of cheap labour. And when China entered the global market in a major way in the second half of the 1990s, its ability to offer economies of scale and very low costs, and its conducting business in international currency, challenged the market shares of other countries, particularly in Central America and South and Southeast Asia.[19]

It has been widely acknowledged that women were the preferred labour force for labour-intensive export production, because their gendered training and identity ensured that they were productive employees, often working long shifts in difficult conditions for relatively low wages with little in the way of non-wage benefits or social protection.[20] The preferred mode of accessing the docile cheap labour of women in developing countries was for transnational corporations (TNCs) to establish subsidiaries in developing countries, mainly in the so called export processing zones (EPZs) set up by governments enthusiastic for the foreign exchange and the employment offered by this new form of export-oriented industrialisation. As the decades of the twentieth century moved on, export production moved beyond the EPZs, as governments established favourable tax and labour regimes, often throughout their territories, which facilitated access to local female labour at minimum cost to the capital employing them.[21]

One particular mode of accessing women's low-cost labour for the production of commodities destined for the markets of developing

countries was the *maquiladoras* – factories located along the
3,000 kilometre border between the USA and Mexico, which follows the transcontinental contours of the Rio Grande. Mexico
is a convenient location for subsidiaries of US companies. The
Mexican government declared the whole of the border territories a
Free Trade Zone, and invested in special 'Industrial Parks' where
foreign companies could rent factory buildings, and gain privileged
access to utilities, communications and water. The workforce,
initially comprising women migrants from the interior provinces,
lived in shanty towns surrounding these zones; in contrast to the
production processes inside the factory, no provision was made for
their housing, transport or other requirements.[22] Meanwhile, the
American management often retained their residency on the other
side of the border, walking daily over the bridges that connect, for
example, San Diego and Tijuana, to work in the burgeoning twin
plants of these border industries.

Whether international manufacturing companies had to travel
just beyond their borders or to the other side of the world, capital
was increasingly mobile, and able to take advantage of the relative immobility of labour, employing workers whose fixed location in a poorer low-wage economy made them amenable towards
the jobs offered by export factories. Over the intervening years,
the story has been complicated, with new internationally traded
products emerging: in addition to manufacturing, horticulture
(fruit and vegetables) is now an important enterprise in developing countries with the appropriate climate – the planting,
weeding and harvesting done by another phalanx of (seasonal
and insecure) nimble-fingered women, to fill the shelves of super-
markets and resorts in North America, Europe, Australasia and
Japan.[23]

Services, too, are now internationalised: for instance, health
care and domestic workers travel from poor countries to work
in the cities of the North and the rich Gulf countries;[24] and in
some cases those seeking care and nursing undertake to travel
themselves to developing countries to obtain the services they

cannot access in their own countries, due either to cost or to the absence of state provision.

A wide range of information and communications technology (ICT) services have also been internationalised, with data entry work being superseded by call centre operators, harnessing the new technologies to access cheap labour in developing countries.

Finally, the mode of international outsourcing based on the utilisation of cheap Third World labour has also changed; whereas in earlier decades such production was largely confined to specific (export processing) industrial zones, this is no longer the case. One reason for this change is that global corporations have switched from the establishment of direct subsidiaries in developing countries, involving contracting local labour in specially designated locations. Now the nature of global competition in supply has become more complicated; market share in consumer outlets in the North is based as much on brand recognition (Nike, Reebok etc.) and the ability to respond in a timely manner to fast-changing fashion trends as it is on price. So many international companies have become 'hollowed out': they no longer directly produce the goods they export in factories that they manage and control; instead they subcontract production to local firms, which produce to the specification and order of the international company. This arrangement shifts the risks down the supply chain to local firms, which have the responsibility to deliver according to deadlines, specification and price; they therefore have to deal with the hiring, management and conditions of local labour involved in that production.

Thus the world of international outsourcing looks very different today to the picture emerging in the 1970s which gave rise to the conception of 'the new international division of labour'; supply chains have become very complex, often reaching below the standard factory in developing countries to a series of informal workshops, and even home-based production, thereby making regulation of labour conditions very difficult to monitor or enforce.[25]

In the context of these sweeping changes in the global economy in recent times, what is so special about the deployment of migrant labour in Thailand's export factories? First, it throws light on a situation where trans-border migrants are being recruited as cheap labour in export plants rather than the more common practice of using internal rural migrants. Second, this is a case where it is the labour rather than the capital that migrates across borders. This contrasts with widespread assumptions that in the modern globalised economy it is capital in the form of finance or direct investment that is the mobile element in the deregulated governance of trade and financial flows. Interestingly, although in recent years there has been considerable academic interest in migration – not just South–North migration but also the movement of people across borders in the global South – little of this analysis has focused on migration for export factory work. Rather, the emphasis has been on migrant workers engaged in agriculture and construction (most of whom are men, though many bring their families with them). Where research has focused on migrant women workers, the main emphasis has been on domestic and care workers, and on sex workers – both voluntary and forced (trafficked women).[26] The fact that the literature largely overlooks migrant workers involved in manufacturing, and as a consequence ignores the circumstances and the care responsibilities of migrant factory workers, is discussed below.

However, Burmese migrant workers in Thailand are not a unique phenomenon. Migrant workers elsewhere have also been drawn to new sectors of production. For example, in China rural migrants in their thousands have met the ever-increasing demand for factory labour, leaving their rural communities to seek jobs in the large factories of the dormitory cities in the south of the country, which has seen an exponential growth in the production of garments, shoes and electronic goods for export markets. Whilst such migrants in China are technically domestic rather than international, they face many of the same challenges encountered by migrant Burmese workers in China: lack of social protection; no entitlement to welfare or social insurance;[27] difficulties in accessing health care for themselves and their children; no right to settle permanently without an ongoing contract of employment; no protection against harsh working conditions and excessive hours.[28] These are problems common to export production workers across the developing world. However, in the case of migrant workers who cross from one state jurisdiction to another, they are compounded by the issue of citizenship and identity, which we will now consider.[29]

Burmese migrant workers: citizenship and entitlement in a hostile world

Migrant factory workers are part of a million-strong army of migrant workers in Thailand who fill the so-called 3D jobs – dirty, dangerous and demeaning – that most Thais, the beneficiaries of significant improvements in education and well-being over recent decades, are not willing to take. But the segregation of migrants within the Thai economy is not just about low-paid, physically exhausting and often unpleasant occupations; it is also about the fact that migrant workers, unlike their Thai counterparts, receive only very limited, and in many cases non-existent, protection from the authorities regarding level of pay and working conditions. Furthermore, they are in the country with, at best, only a temporary state permit, have no job security and are therefore unable to organise to improve their situation. This of course is the case with migrant workers all over the world, especially those without the documentation that confers the right to be in the country. But for women factory workers, issues concerning gender and reproduction complicate the situation further: their dual position as workers and as women – as daughters, sisters, wives and mothers – brings into sharp relief their particular vulnerability.

Regulation of so-called 'irregular migrants' is discussed in detail in Chapter 2, but in outline the situation is as follows. Since the mid-1990s Thailand has responded to demands by its own manufacturers for controlled access to cheap labour from poorer neighbouring countries, namely Laos, Cambodia and Burma. Access was until recently controlled through a specially designed programme that offered migrants temporary registration as 'irregular workers' and a permit on payment of a fee, with an arrangement to work for a designated employer. Registration as an irregular worker did not give a migrant the right to remain in the country legally; rather, in effect it confirmed their illegal status, but conferred a stay of deportation, so that technically the worker was safe from any action by the immigration police until the registration expired. This registration exercise continued sporadically until 2010, but has now been replaced by the issuing of temporary passports and work permit under bilateral Memoranda of Understanding (MOUs) with neighbouring governments, which require would-be migrants to obtain a nationality verification document – in effect a passport – in their country of origin before travelling to Thailand. This document enables migrant workers to register for a two-year period, renewable for a further two years. The permits are in general only valid for the worker herself or himself; family members, including children born to workers already in the country, are not included.

Although registration and the current passport system apply to cross-border migrants from Cambodia and Laos as well as Burma, historically the majority have come from Burma, in response to the political and economic oppression in the country. However, as we detail in Chapter 2, only a minority of Burmese workers actually obtain official permits; it is estimated that some 60 per cent of the total number working lack such documentation, often with the collusion of employers. Even those who hold the documentation are not guaranteed protection from hostility or harassment by factory owners, the authorities or the general Thai population.

It should be said that this policy of controlling temporary migrant workers is not unique to Thailand; in much of the rest of Asia, foreign workers are similarly tightly controlled, particularly in the middle-income expanding economies of India and China. Thailand's mixture of policies, which appear at once to deter, control and facilitate employers' access to cheap labour, is significant on two counts: one, because in some sectors, including export industries, migrants constitute such a large part of the labour force; two, because the migrants are virtually invisible to policymakers as well as absent from general debates on present and future economic strategy.

As a consequence of their shadow existence, migrant workers very often end up without any official identity or citizenship either in their country of origin or in Thailand. As we discovered, many of these workers left their homes without any official documentation from the local authorities in their home towns or villages; and, given the system of temporary registration and work permits, only a minority possess any legal documentation relating to their presence in Thailand. Although the introduction of the temporary passport system under the MOU procedures is officially designed to ensure that all migrant workers carry identity documents from their place of origin, this is proving impossible for many Burmese migrants. First, the cost of returning home to obtain such documentation is prohibitive; second, to make such a journey would risk the loss of their job; third, it is widely reported that the Burmese authorities are taking a close interest in households with migrant workers, particularly in ethnic minority provinces, targeting such families with demands for forced labour, tithes, taxation, food and other support for the armed forces, as well as increasing surveillance of those suspected of political activity against the regime. According to recent research by Human Rights Watch, 'Burmese migrants in Thailand cited the following among their reasons for leaving Burma: forced labour, extortion, arbitrary taxation, confiscation of land and property, and movement restrictions that negatively impact villagers' agricultural work'; hence 'sending one or several members of the family to seek work in Thailand and send back remittances is thus best understood as a survival strategy for many Burmese families.'[30]

Yet the Burmese migrants in Thailand often find themselves in a hostile environment 'between the Tiger and the Crocodile'.[31]

Whilst for many the life they have escaped in Burma can rightly be described as a situation of human rights abuse, there is ample evidence that what they face in Thailand often adds up to the same thing. Not only has Thailand exhibited a long-standing hostility to people from non-Thai ethnicities, including so-called 'hill tribes' native to their own territory;[32] there is also a clear gap between, on the one hand, official policy positions and statements by the government, and, on the other, widespread corruption and profiteering at the level of the police and immigration authorities. Our interviews document multiple examples of collusion between factory owners, the Thai and Burmese agents who organise the smuggling of workers from Burma to locations in Thailand, the police and the immigration service; these findings are confirmed by Human Rights Watch and other reports. Such collusion ranges from simple actions intended to evade the application of the law to severe cases that involve harassment, imprisonment, rape and murder.

On one occasion, a sunny afternoon in July 2007, our team watched with incredulity as, some 200 metres downstream from the Thai–Burmese Friendship Bridge in Mae Sot, in a period of thirty minutes some fifteen boats packed with young Burmese women crossed the border and landed on Thai territory. The women stepped out of the boat with their colourful umbrellas to avoid the sun and made their way to the many low-end riverside garment factories in Mae Sot to continue with their work. Our Burmese team members were told by the women they spoke to that they had been sent by the factory management to the other side of the river for 'an afternoon's shopping' following a tip-off from the Mae Sot police. We were told that the local police had been informed by their colleagues in Bangkok that there was to be a factory inspection, so the management had thought it prudent to remove the (mainly unregistered) migrant workers that afternoon; but once they had received the all-clear (via the ubiquitous mobile phone) the women were free to return to work.

Migrant workers suffer multiple forms of abuse and repression. Many remain in debt to the 'carriers' that arranged their journey from home, or to the agents who secured them access to their first employer, to a sum many times the level of their monthly earnings, which makes resistance to exploitative working conditions impossible. Reports from NGOs working with the migrant community, supported by researchers' interviews, detail ongoing abuse, including illegal imprisonment, violence and beating, sexual assault, and in some cases homicide.[33] There are also well-documented accounts of apparently orchestrated arrangements that share the spoils of fines, bribes and other payments extracted illegally from the migrants workers. At the official level the Thai government continues to make public commitments to guarantee the rights of migrant workers in its country. But, as later chapters in this book demonstrate, this is sadly not generally the case on the ground.

However, it is not just in the matter of labour rights abuses that migrant workers face discrimination in Thailand. Given the number of young women workers who are or become mothers in the course of their work in Thailand, the issue of citizenship for both adult workers and their children is of extreme importance. It has been estimated officially that there are currently over 100,000 stateless and migrant children in Thailand.[34] Although the government has frequently pledged to honour its commitment to providing 'education for all' children regardless of their migrant or nationality status,[35] most children of migrants are still subject to exclusion and discrimination, as detailed in Chapter 5. In other areas of their lives, women workers strive to balance their multiple obligations to their families both in Burma and in Thailand, and to forge a future for themselves and their children. But their lack of citizenship means not just the absence of labour rights and social protection as workers, but also their gendered exclusion from the entitlement to personal security, health and education facilities, and the rights to family life and to buy and own property. The story of these workers throws into relief the specific gendered nature of their experiences, beyond the general documentation of labour exploitation and abuse common to men and women workers in Thailand and elsewhere.

Who cares? Burmese women in Thailand
as carers and workers

As indicated above, most recent scholarship and research on women's migration in the contemporary global economy have been closely concerned with the growing trend for women migrants from low-wage developing countries to migrate to developed countries, taking jobs in the domestic, health or care sectors which substitute for women's work in the public or private sphere. This has been termed the 'global care chain', which is defined by its originator Arlie Hochschild as 'a series of personal links between people across the globe based on the paid or unpaid work of caring'.[36] This model of transnational care labour embodied in the global care chain literature is one in which a migrant care worker takes on as paid work the family caring responsibilities of women in richer countries, which often implies that the migrant leaves her own care responsibilities, particularly for her own children, to unpaid female family members in her country of origin. Other writers have extended this model of internationalisation of production and migration to include a broader range of care work, such as care of the elderly in non-domestic care homes and facilities, and a wide range of health care.[37] Like previous models of the 'new internationalisation of labour',[38] the global care chain concept focuses on North–South transmissions of labour and value, and ignores South–South migration and mobility.

Our study of Burmese women workers in Thailand is a vivid example of the complexities of the trans-border care responsibilities and strategies of all migrant workers, whether or not they are employed directly as domestic or care workers in their destination country. Indeed for Burmese women employed in factories in Thailand, the challenge of managing their domestic responsibilities, particularly concerning pregnancy, childbirth and childcare, were as pressing as those relating to workplace issues and abuses. In each of the three research locations of our study, women were constantly juggling their different options and duties in relation to their parents at home, to their siblings and children in Thailand, and to themselves and their future with regard to identity, citizenship and future employment opportunities.

Those in Mae Sot had a wider range of options, which involved frequent changes in arrangements; newborns and small children were frequently cared for by grandparents and other family members, who were brought (illegally) across the border; and as circumstances changed, children were sent back to the workers' home villages to be looked after, and sent to school by relatives there. Some brave souls struggled to keep their children with them in the town, sharing the responsibility with their working partners, siblings or friends.

In the central site of Samut Prakhan frequent changes in childcare arrangements were more difficult. It was hard to smuggle children back to Burma over such a distant border, though we did hear quite horrific reports of small babies being placed in the hands of commercial carriers, who had to sedate them in order to make the long and arduous journey to the interior. It is harder for working mothers in Samut Prakhan to hide from the authorities, and many women, especially those with registration documents, were more likely to keep their children with them even though they faced an uphill battle to secure adequate housing, health care and education for them.

In Three Pagodas Pass, which has recently seen growth in the number of export factories, most migrant workers arranged for their children to be cared for by family members located on the Burmese side of the border, and to attend local Burmese schools. Nevertheless, it was quite common for workers to bring babies and infants with them, particularly when tight production schedules required workers to sleep overnight in the factories rather than return to their lodgings across the border. Chapter 5 sets out in detail the complexities of the decisions and arrangements that are necessary for migrant women workers to continue to earn wages in the factories in Thailand. This study therefore contributes to addressing the gaps in the current literature, which, by focusing entirely on either the workplace experiences of factory labour or the work and responsibilities of migrant care workers, ignores entirely the gendered care responsibilities of those from developing countries who are employed in non-care sectors of the economy.

Shifting terrain: Burmese migrant women's responses to economic and political change

This book was prepared at a moment of political and economic uncertainty in both Burma and Thailand. The military regime in Burma staged a referendum in the wake of the devastating Cyclone Nargis in 2008 to approve a new constitution, which promises very small steps towards a degree of participation in the country.[39] Elections, with minimum and controlled political activity, were held in November 2010, followed by the release of Aung San Suu Kyi, leader of the National League for Democracy (NLD) party.[40] Although the opposition party has now agreed to participate in future elections, and its leader has declared her willingness to stand for president, there has as yet been only limited change in the control by the military government of economic and political life in the country; meanwhile refugees and migrants continue to enter Thailand – and other neighbouring countries, including Bangladesh and China – in search of a better futures for themselves and their children.

Thailand is itself experiencing political uncertainty. Although the non-democratically elected regime of prime minister Abhisit Vejajiva was replaced by Yinluck Sinawatra following the general election in July 2011, instability remains. There is continuing unrest in the border provinces in the south, ongoing border conflicts with Cambodia, and uncertainty about the health of the popular but ageing monarch King Bhumibol Adulyadej. Political divisions have been exacerbated by the aftermath of the worst floods in half a century; these have produced direct questioning of the competence of the prime minister, who is the younger sister of the former populist leader Thaksin Shinawatra, who was ousted by a military coup in 2006. Nevertheless, according to *The Economist* the Thai economy made a good recovery following the global financial crisis in 2008/9, and industrialists, particularly in export sectors, have reaped the benefits of a sustained and rising growth rate, though this might well be affected by the economic and political consequences of the floods. In any event, the demand for migrant workers is likely to continue.[41]

This book offers a rare insight into the lives of those workers at a critical time for both their country of origin and their current country of destination. In spite of the continuing problems and deprivations suffered by migrant workers, we are also witnessing a resoluteness in the face of uncertainty. As Chapter 6 demonstrates, it is significant that even at the height of the economic crisis women migrant workers in particular were committed to remaining in Thailand – to fulfilling their obligations to their families by sending remittances back home and maintaining the option to continue to work in Thailand to secure their futures and those of their children. In many ways their fate reflects that of the two countries between which their lives are suspended; their stories highlight the challenges that exist to a proper understanding of the importance of their waged work for the Thai economy as well as for themselves, their families and their communities. But the book also throws light on the very particular experiences of women who are at once workers, daughters and mothers, and on the courage that is required to juggle the complexities and contradictions of these dual roles.

2

Thailand's industrialisation and labour migration policies

Thailand's industrialisation before and after the Asian financial crisis of the 1990s

In the 1970s and 1980s Thailand was among the fastest growing and most successful developing countries in the world; it achieved impressive progress in poverty reduction, and raised education and living standards for its population, while overseeing a large population shift from the countryside to urban areas.[1] However, by the 1980s growth had stalled, due in part to the global recession provoked by the oil crisis. It was during this period that the government switched to an export-oriented industrialisation strategy, largely based on the inflow of foreign investment from Japan as well as other Asian NICs and Western countries. By the mid-1990s, manufactures, including garments, textiles, footwear and electronics, accounted for over 80 per cent of total exports, replacing agriculture as the leading sector of the economy. Thailand followed a standard World Bank-approved export-led strategy, enhanced by a decentralisation policy which encouraged larger export factories to locate in the northern and southern industrial estates (similar to export processing zones).[2] As the industrial sector grew, so did its workforce, which had more than doubled by the mid-1990s.[3] The fortunes of the labour movement in Thailand reflected the growth in industrial production and employment: following years of repression during the anti-communist counter-insurgency in the 1970s, the unions became stronger from the early 1990s, and began to work with other pro-democracy civil society organisations. The number of registered trade unions multiplied from 430 in 1984 to 931 in 1994, and labour disputes more than doubled over the same period, even though – in line with many other countries in the region – the rate of unionisation remained low, accounting for only 2 per cent of the labour force, and 11 per cent of industrial workers, in 2002.[4] The number of workers covered by social security also remains low, accounting for less than a quarter of the 36 million-strong labour force by 2006. The government did begin to take stock of growing labour discontent and introduced a range of measures, including the Workmen's Compensation Fund (a workers' accident compensation scheme), as well as raising the minimum wage. However, only a small fraction of the formal workforce benefited from these measures; those working in small and medium enterprises – at least half the registered workforce – and the vast majority of migrant workers still worked for very low pay and without protection.

Meanwhile the Thai economy was being buffeted by competition in the global market and the growth rate of exports declined throughout the 1990s. By 1997, when the Thai baht depreciated sharply following its flotation, many export sectors, particularly those dependent on imported raw materials, were thrown into crisis.[5] Output fell sharply in agriculture, construction and manufacturing, and there were large-scale redundancies, particularly in the textile and garment sectors, where over a million workers were laid off between 1998 and 1999, of which the overwhelming proportion – over 90 per cent – were women.[6]

The crisis – part of the general Asian crisis of the late 1990s – led to a restructuring of Thai industry. According to the International Labour Organization (ILO),

As part of cost-cutting measures and efforts to enhance competitiveness, firms are increasingly operating with a small core of wage employees with regular terms and conditions (formal employment) based in a fixed formal workplace and a growing periphery of 'nonstandard' or 'atypical' and often informal workers in different types of workplaces scattered over different locations.[7]

Meanwhile the bulk of the government's policies to mitigate the negative effects of the crisis were directed at male workers in rural areas.[8] There was a widespread assumption that retrenched workers would return to their rural villages, and that they and their families would be re-absorbed into their home communities. Many thousands of workers did return, though opportunities for women were restricted. The government extended some of the benefits for retrenched formal sector workers, including severance payments and social security benefits,[9] but once again those who worked for smaller enterprises and in the informal sector, where most women industrial workers were employed, were largely ignored.

Following the crisis, the Thai economy recovered fairly rapidly, averaging 4.5 per cent growth between 1995 and 2005, though per capita income did not recover to its pre-crisis level until 2005. In the meantime Thai domestic capital asserted its political and economic interests, backing a new political party, Thai Rak Thai (Thais Love Thailand), headed by Thaksin Shinawatra, which won power in 2001 on the basis of a populist contract that offered substantial investment in social welfare and rural poverty reduction. Although there was significant investment in infrastructure, Thai industrialists serving the domestic market were largely protected from foreign competition by a range of trade agreements and government policies. But those competing in export markets, particularly the garment and textile industry, still needed the basis of cheap labour, in an environment increasingly dominated by the capacity of other Asian countries – not just China but also Vietnam and Bangladesh – to undercut them with lower labour costs and higher productivity.[10]

Employment in the textile and garment sectors began to decline after 1995;[11] however, official statistics show that it is still one of the major sources of employment in Thailand, estimated at 1.1 million in 2006, some 20 per cent of total manufacturing employment. Given the complexities of subcontracting within Thailand to informal and home-based workshops, and the increase in the employment of unregistered migrant labour, the actual number of workers in this section might well be two or three times higher than estimated. The sector continues to employ predominantly female labour – at least 80 per cent of all workers. One of the strategies that has helped maintain levels of production and employment in Thailand's export industries is the policy of searching for cheaper labour within the country's borders: moving production out of higher-wage central areas to the north-east and northern border provinces where wage rates are lower, and employing cheaper workers, both Thai women working in home-based or informal workshops, and migrant workers from neighbouring countries, especially Burma.

Decentralisation of industry[12]

Industrialists, particularly those involved in export subcontracting in the garment sector, are well aware of the utility of accessing cheap migrant workers in order to make their products competitive in the international market. The case of 'Bed and Bath Prestige', a Thai textile and garment conglomerate, is a good illustration of this strategy. Bed and Bath subcontracted production work in central and provincial Thailand for a range of overseas customers including Nike, Adidas and Levi's, and for a number of sports and college outlets in the USA. A former manger was quoted thus:

> I think Bed & Bath will find their business solution through the use of sub-contractors in Mae Sot. They cannot continue in Bangkok because each order received from overseas buyers only generates small profits considering the high wages in Bangkok. Thus the company plans to distribute orders to sub-contractors in Mae Sot. Their wages are low and other expenses are also very low, this is the only way

the company can survive and make profits. And in the future it is possible that the company will open factories there because there are plenty of cheap Burmese workers.[13]

Thailand initiated a policy of decentralisation of industry before the 1997 financial crisis, avowedly as a strategy to improve international relations by encouraging economic development by its less developed neighbours, and to even out development and living standards between Bangkok and less prosperous areas of the country. The idea of 'special economic zones' in border areas was included in the seventh National Social and Economic Development Plan (1992–96), which announced the promotion of cross-border trade and the creation of new economic zones in the provinces of Chiang Rai, Tak, Nongkai, Mukdahan and Ubon Ratchathani, and this became the key industrial decentralisation strategy in the subsequent plan (1997–2001). The Thai government offered tax and other incentives to encourage industry to move out of Bangkok, and lower minimum wages were set for border provinces, a policy still in force today. In 2011, the minimum wage is highest in the central provinces of Bangkok and Samut Prakan (205 baht per day), a third higher than the official daily minimum wage of 153 baht in Tak province where Mae Sot is located, offering considerable incentives for factories based on labour-intensive production.

The development of trans-border economic activity – both production and commerce – reflects Thailand's aspiration to economic leadership in the Greater Mekong subregion. In addition to various trade agreements, Thailand has established an economic development cooperation fund, which has granted soft-loan finance for infrastructure projects, particularly in Burma where Thailand continues to be a major investor.

The Bagan declaration[14] of November 2003, signed by four countries – Burma/Myanmar, Thailand, Laos and Cambodia – set out the terms of bilateral and regional development cooperation. In addition the ACMECS (Ayeyarwady–Chaophraya–Mekong Economic Cooperation Strategy), also called ECS (Economic Cooperation Strategy), was signed in 2003, envisioning a series of sister cities

that would offer mutual assistance to achieve economic growth and
improve social problems, a concept which owed its genesis to the
twin cities on the US–Mexico border,[15] which had benefited from
US investment in the development of infrastructure in Mexico, and,
as we noted in Chapter 1, supported the establishment of free-trade
zones and industrial parks. Thai logic echoed the policy objectives
of border development in North America – both to stem the flow of
illegal immigrants to the richer country and to create employment
and foreign exchange earnings for the poorer country.

> [T]his economic gap, especially the income gap between Thailand
> and the neighbouring countries, results in the inflow of illegal
> foreign workers into Thailand and becomes the main cause of drug
> inflow and various crimes. ... In order to solve these issues, the Thai
> government is now planning to set up special economic zones in
> border areas to relocate agriculture and labour intensive industries
> from the centre to there and to utilize the cheap labour and re-
> sources of the neighbouring countries and finally to stop the inflow
> of the illegal migrants and the relevant problems. [16]

The idea was for the border special economic zones to incorpo-
rate a series of incentives for the (re)location of industry, including
the right to employ migrant workers.[17] However, the policy has
never been implemented as such, although provincial governors
do have the discretion to implement specific regulations in their
jurisdictions, and have introduced in several provinces measures
such as the ban on migrant workers using mobile phones, riding
motorcycles or assembling in meetings of more than five persons.[18]
There have been investments in transportation infrastructure in
response to the growth of manufacturing factories employing
migrant workers from Burma in Tak province. Mae Sot airport
was modernised and reopened, and improvements were made to
roads between Mae Sot and the Tak provincial centre. At one point
there were plans for the construction of an industrial estate on
the Burmese side of the border, but these have been suspended
in light of the political instability in both Thailand and Burma,
although there are indications that the idea of such developments

on both sides of the border at Mae Sot are being revived. There are also indications that the plans for an export trade and production zone in Mae Sot are being reconsidered. Whilst the overt purpose of investments and incentives for the decentralisation of industry in Thailand are strictly related to economic development, they are also considered central to minimising the problems relating to the illegal migration of workers from Burma. It is hoped that the proposed special economic zones will help contain migrant workers within the border areas, stopping the constant flow of new migrants towards the more prosperous central provinces where they are much harder to control.

Although the Thai government has encouraged direct investment in Burma, the few industrialists who established manufacturing facilities on the Myawaddy side of the border have not been successful and have subsequently relocated their production facilities back to Mae Sot where there is better infrastructure and much greater certainty concerning government policy and support.[19] There are reports that a number of Burmese companies which previously operated from the Burmese capital of Yangon are relocating to the Thai border towns of Kanchanaburi and Mae Sot.[20]

Indeed the derelict remains of a failed factory investment on the Burmese side are still clearly visible across the river from Mae Sot. According to local industrialists a Thai entrepreneur built a garment factory on the Burmese side of the border, hoping it would be easier to access cheap Burmese workers. However, he was quickly dismayed by the level of bureaucracy involved in running an industrial establishment within Burma as well as the unforeseen additional payments he was obliged to make, and relocated back to Mae Sot within a few years.

It is not just the Tak border town of Mae Sot that has benefited from the trend in location of export manufacturing plants on the border with Burma in order to take advantage of the supply of cheap labour. There has also been considerable growth of such factories at Three Pagodas Pass in Kanchanaburi province, where there is relatively little restriction on the constant trans-border movements of workers from the Burmese to the Thai side of the border. The wage rate here is even lower than that prevailing in Mae Sot. It is also likely that there will be other locations for border industries on the southern border between Burma and Thailand as well as on the borders with neighbouring Laos and Cambodia. A more detailed account of all three of the towns, including the non-border districts of Prapadaeng in Samut Prakan province and Bang Kunthien in Bangkok municipality, in which we carried out this research, is given in Chapter 3. A finding of our study was that the regimes developed by the Thai government both to facilitate the utilisation of cheap Burmese workers in export factories and at the same time to control their conditions of entry, residence, employment, mobility and entitlements determine that these workers' lives in Thailand continue to be difficult and give rise to exploitation, which rarely gets raised in discussion of Thailand's economic development strategy.

Demand for and control of migrant labour: regulating the irregular

Demand for migrant labour and the economic crisis

The garment and textile industries, which have universally been sectors where women workers are concentrated, are at the heart of the demand for cheap migrant labour in Thailand, and it is these sectors that have responded to incentives and opportunities to shift production to cheaper border areas. Mae Sot in Tak province, in particular, has witnessed a dramatic increase in both the number of factories and the number of workers employed.[21]

Although industrialists were enthusiastic about the new policies, anxiety about the effects of hiring cheap migrants persisted, with many commentators reminding the government that concessions should be confined to border areas so as not to distort employment and wage structures in the wider national labour market:

It is believed that hiring more irregular migrants in this sector may distort the employment and wage structure of the labour market as a whole. Therefore, the allowance should be an area-specific issue in this sector. Only establishments in the provinces, along the border (or those currently under the BOI's promotional privilege) should be permitted to employ irregular migrants but definitely not those in the inner provinces of Thailand. [22]

Growth in border industries has continued, although more recent data indicate that there was a slowdown in growth in 2008/9 as Thailand absorbed the shocks of the global financial crisis of 2007/8. In 2009, the Thai Garment Manufacturers' Association (TGMA) complained of severe labour shortages, and suggested that the garment industry in Thailand was now looking to invest in neighbouring countries. Vallop Vitanakorn, the TGMA secretary general, told the *Bangkok Post*[23] that 'right now we have a shortage of 50,000 to 60,000 people in the industry and this will definitely reach 60,000 by next year.' Certainly Thailand's reliance on cheap migrant labour for its export industries seems set to continue. But at the same time there is a strong desire to contain such workers in specific parts of the country where they will not be able to affect – or infect – the rest of the economy and the labour force, much of which had continued to enjoy rising living standards. This was especially true of the Thaksin regime in the period 2001–06, which successfully targeted social and economic expenditure on rural areas. This meant that a relocation of industry to rural areas in search of cheap labour was no longer a feasible strategy for Thai industrialists. Even during the period of the 1990s' crisis, rural Thais were unwilling to work for the low wages paid by the border factories, having grown accustomed to a better standard of living, which has been enhanced by sustained improvements in education and the extension of government health and other services.

Thai workers have also been somewhat cushioned from the effects of the crisis compared to migrant workers, with schemes to retrain retrenched workers returning to their villages of origin, combined with credit for those wanting to start small businesses and support for peri-urban enterprises linked to the marketing of agricultural products and handicrafts, in the context of the 'Buy Thai, Thai Help Thai' policies. New regulations offering increased severance pay and unemployment benefits for Thai workers in the formal sector also aimed to help mitigate the impact of the crisis on the Thai industrial workforce, although women in informal employment were left out of these schemes.

There was no cushion for migrant workers, whether they were registered or not. The immediate response of the Thai government after the crisis was to mitigate the impact in terms of rising unemployment for Thai workers by repatriating 'illegal, alien workers'. In 1998, 300,000 foreign workers (mainly Burmese) were deported, in spite of protests from both local employers and human rights activists. Thai local politicians, who were also owners of business enterprises that had employed migrant workers, did not support the repatriation policy, which was also strongly opposed by rice millers and fishing-sector entrepreneurs. Moreover, unemployed Thais were mainly concentrated in the central regions of the country, whilst foreign workers tended to be more dispersed and difficult for the authorities to round up. In any case, it was found that those who were forcibly removed tended to return illegally to Thailand as soon as they got the opportunity. In the end, the repatriation policy was abandoned, with support from local exporters; the state went back to its previous, more tolerant, position on the recruitment of foreign workers.[24]

It is a widely held view in Thailand that the much publicised repatriation of migrant workers in 1997-98 was a political exercise to persuade the Thai population that the government was committed to protect the employment and rights of its own citizens, in line with a surge of populist nationalism that followed the economic shocks of the late 1990s. The early stages of the crisis

[p]rovoked two historical comparisons. The first was to the defeat of Ayutthaya by the Burmese in 1767. The conventional shorthand for this event, Sia Krung (the fall of the city), lent itself easily to

metaphors of an urban economic crisis. The second reference was to the period of colonial threats to Siam's existence in the 1890s.[25]

The popular movements that emerged after the crisis were considered to be 'focus[ed] inward rather than outward' – not necessarily in the sense of rejecting external forces, but more to cultivate Thainess and a sense of community.[26] That period saw a number of popular manifestations in support of this. For instance, people were encouraged to donate foreign currency, or even gold or silver jewellery, to help pay off the national debt as part of the *pha pa chuay chat* (donation to help the nation), which was championed by well-known Buddhist monks. The 'Thai Help Thai' campaign was designed to promote the production and consumption of goods made in Thailand to help the country weather the financial crisis. Although nationalism did not develop into an aggressive political force, as in other countries, these pro-Thai nationalistic sentiments formed the context of public opinion in 1997–98 when a very visible policy of deporting migrant workers was pursued.

However, return was not a viable option for many of the migrant workers facing the threat of deportation. In 1997 the Burmese economy deteriorated in the face of a number of external shocks. Not only were the country's trade with and investment in neighbouring countries hit by the Asian financial crisis; it also faced a recently instituted ban by the USA on new investment. The resultant rise in urban unemployment, along with government measures such as the forced selling of agricultural products much below market price, meant that returning home was not a feasible option for migrants, whose motivation to work in Thailand was as much economic as it was political.[27]

The 2008 global financial crisis did not have such a devastating effect on Thailand as the previous crisis, though 2009 was marked by bankruptcies, lay-offs and reductions in the length of the working day. For example, it was reported that during January fifty business enterprises shut down and at least 25,000 factory workers were laid off, with double that number having to accept wage cuts due to decreased working hours. Once again the government chose to focus on migrant workers to indicate its support for the Thai population; in January 2009 labour minister Paitoon Kaewthong announced that the registration of thousands of foreign workers – a scheme that had just been overhauled – would be delayed to protect Thai jobs.[28]

Migrant labour management

Registration has long served as the policy tool to access and control migration of workers in Thailand. Because of the fluid and often clandestine nature of migration to Thailand from Burma and elsewhere, it is difficult to establish any accurate measure of the numbers involved. In addition, a system dubbed 'regulating the irregular' has been operated: the practice of registering illegal migrants not by making them legal, but by regularising their status so that they have an official stay of deportation for a given period of time, during which they are allowed to be employed provided they conform to certain conditions concerning the kind of jobs they do, the employers they work for, and the localities they work in.

The most frequently cited estimate of the number of migrant workers in Thailand is that of the Office of National Economic and Social Development Board (NESDB), which calculated that in 2003 there were 920,379, of whom 568,000 – just under 62 per cent – were registered. Although there are also migrants from Cambodia and Laos, which have borders with Thailand, it is generally agreed that over 80 per cent of both registered and unregistered migrants are from Burma. Sources give different figures for the numbers of Burmese currently living in Thailand. One estimate for 2009–10 is 1.3 million, a figure based on those who have indicated their desire to register under the current nationality verification procedures; however, migrant organisations such as the MAP Foundation put the number at between 2 and 3 million. Migrant workers are concentrated in and around Bangkok and other main cities, and in border areas. NESDB estimated that of the total number of migrant workers from Burma, 45 per cent are agriculture and fishery workers, 22 per cent are factory workers, 17 per cent general workers and 16 per cent household (domestic) workers.

Thailand was formerly a source of migrant workers, but in recent years has become the largest receiving country of the Greater Mekong Subregion (GMS) area. The country has ratified various agreements related to migrant labour, including fourteen ILO conventions on labour standards, and is a signatory of the 2004 ILO Resolution Concerning a Fair Deal for Migrant Workers in the Global Economy and of the 2007 ASEAN Declaration on the Protection and Promotion of the Rights of Migrant Workers. But it has declined to sign ILO conventions that protect the rights of migrant labour, including the Migration for Employment Convention (Revised) No. 97, the Migrant Workers (Supplementary Provisions) Convention No. 143, the Migrant Workers Recommendation No. 151, and the United Nations International Convention on the Protection of the Rights of all Migrant Workers and Members of their families.[29] On the other hand, Thailand has been active in the anti-human trafficking field and has signed a raft of international conventions and agreements, including the United Nations Convention on Transnational Organized Crime in 2001, and has ratified ILO Convention No. 29 and No. 105 on Forced Labour, and the ILO Convention No. 182 on the Worst Forms of Child Labour. It has also signed the ASEAN Declaration on Transnational Crime (1997) and the ASEAN Declaration Against Trafficking in Persons Particularly Women and Children (2004). Thailand is active in the Coordinated Mekong Ministerial Initiative against Trafficking (COMMIT).

However, anti-trafficking measures tend to obscure discussion about the need to protect the interests of migrant workers who go willingly to Thailand to seek employment:

> The persistent focus on rehabilitation and repatriation has provoked concerns among migrant advocates that the key issues of regularizing labour migration and providing labour protection to migrant workers in Thailand may not be adequately addressed through a

trafficking framework and should be covered by specified immigration legislation. ... It remains a question how the enforcement of these measures will differentiate between 'trafficked' and 'smuggled' migrant workers, and what degree of exploitation at work will be considered trafficking.[30]

Moreover, the measures enacted by the Thai government since 1992 concerning the registration of temporary migrant workers from neighbouring countries have been seen by many as protecting the economic and political interests of Thai employers and politicians rather than those of the migrant workers themselves.[31]

The legal basis for the temporary hiring of low-skilled migrant workers is found in Section 12 of the Alien Employment Act B.E. 2521 and Section 17 of Immigration Act B.C. 2522, which grant the Ministry of Interior discretion under 'special circumstances' to exempt migrant workers from being deported during the period of their registration. But whether registered or not, migrant workers in Thailand are regarded as 'aliens' – that is, they are persons who do not have Thai nationality.

In the years after 1996 illegal migrant workers in Thailand were subject to a series of registration exercises. In 2009 a nationality verification scheme was introduced. This system, drawn up as an MOU with the governments of neighbouring countries, requires workers to obtain nationality verification and a temporary passport from their place of origin before applying – and paying for – registration to stay in Thailand, as well as a work permit. These registration documents, which are linked to employment, permitting migrants in specified provinces to work with particular employers for a specified period, have become increasingly restrictive over time.

The first registration of irregular migrants took place in 1992; this allowed the registration of migrant workers along the Thai-Burmese border, and it was extended in 1993 by a decree which permitted the registration of illegal migrant workers in twenty-two coastal provinces (out of a total seventy-six). Under the 1992/3 policies, registered workers were able to receive a permit to work in

Thailand for four years, though this had to be renewed each year. The system was extended to migrants from Laos and Cambodia, in addition to those from Burma, in 1996 and the number of provinces included was increased to forty-three, and the number of permitted economic sectors (deemed 3Ds and therefore labour shortage sectors) was increased to eleven, comprising agriculture, fisheries, fishery-related activities, construction, domestic work, salt fields, timber mills, brick-making, production of fish-related products, and 'other production activities' (which include garment and other manufacturing processes).

The 1996 registration was considered a success and the government reportedly increased its determination to enforce its system and deport all unregistered migrants. After the economic crisis of 1997 the Thai government prioritised policies that supported employment for Thai nationals, as discussed above, and widespread retrenchment of migrant workers, as well as an increase in their forced removal. In Mae Sot police were reported to have raided a number of garment factories in 1999 and repeatedly removed unauthorised migrants, leading to hundreds of complaints regarding a shortage of workers. In January 2000, the Tak province Industrial Council complained that Thais were not willing to replace the migrants who had been removed; according to the Council some 20,000 were deported but only 6,000 Thais applied for their jobs.[32]

The new registration exercise in 2001 extended the possibility of migrants working in all industries and all provinces. But it included a condition that the migrant worker had to be registered with a particular employer, who would be liable for the fee payment of 3,250 baht (equivalent to £46 at that time). The fee included 1,200 baht health insurance for state hospitals, 900 baht for a six-month work permit, 150 baht for an ID card, and a 1,000 baht bond. In addition migrants were obliged to renew their work permits after six months, for which they were required to pay a further 900 baht. With a 300 baht health fee, the total payable amounted to 4,450 baht for a twelve-month period. The 2001 registration

FIGURE 2.1   Registered migrants 1997–2008 (million)

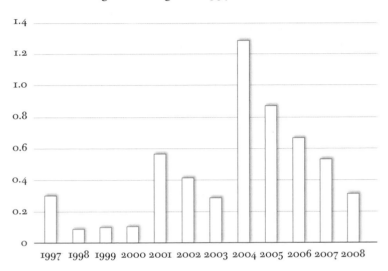

Sources Sciortino and Punpuing 2009; MAP Foundation website; Ministry of Labour website.

exercise was followed by renewals in 2002 and 2003. In 2004 the government acceded to the increasingly vociferous concerns of the police and security agencies, and changed the framework for managing irregular migration, which led to the strengthening of border controls and the granting of enhanced police powers. Given the equally strongly expressed demand from employers, who claimed that the labour deficit exceeded 1.5 million, a new registration exercise was authorised, which set a cost of 3,800 baht for a full twelve-month registration.

Subsequent registration exercises in 2005 and 2006 in effect only allowed the re-registration of existing workers with named employers. In 2006 only 220,892 workers renewed or registered. But later that year the system was modified to allow a currently unregistered worker the right to register with a new employer should their employer die, not pay for work done, engage in unfair dismissal, cease trading or change business; this led to a further 460,000 workers being registered. The 2006 registration only permits the migrant worker her/himself to remain in Thailand, unlike the measures enacted in 2001 and 2004, which allowed accompanying family members such as spouses, parents and children to be registered. The numbers of workers registered between 1997 and 2008 are shown in Figure 2.1.

The 2006 *coup d'état* which ousted the Thaksin government brought about a change in registration policy. In 2007, policy was restricted to the re-registration of existing migrants and a new scheme for workers in five southern provinces to meet labour shortages in the tourist, construction and fishing sectors. After 2006, it was clear that provincial governments were exercising their autonomy in terms of restricting the movements and liberties of migrant workers within their jurisdictions. The first provincial decree was enacted in Phuket province on grounds of 'national security': this forbade migrant workers to own or drive a car, ride a motorcycle, use a mobile phone or travel outside their dormitory between 8.00 or 10.00 p.m. and 6 a.m. Rayong province imposed a similar decree, which also prohibited migrants from gathering in groups of five or more unless they were working. By the end of 2007 similar restrictions were in force in five other provinces.

Such restrictions were in line with the martial law imposed after the *coup d'état* in September 2006, as well as the harder line taken by the military government on the control of migrant workers, who were seen as alien and polluting.[33]

The restoration of parliamentary rule in 1997 had initiated a refocusing of Thailand's external strategies, particularly in terms of her role in the Greater Mekong subregion, as well as ASEAN. This required new and more coherent policies on managing migrant workers from neighbouring countries. Negotiations were put in train to sign bilateral MOUs with Laos, Cambodia and Burma/Myanmar, which were officially signed in 2002/3. These agreements introduced the nationality verification process, referred to above, which required migrant workers to first obtain

documentation from their own governments which validated their
identity and permitted them to travel out of the country (which
is referred to as a 'passport' but is actually only valid for travel
overland to Thailand), before they could apply for registration
and work permits. Burma was somewhat tardy in implementing
this agreement, which meant that several temporary renewals of
the existing registration regime were required. By the time the
agreement was officially ratified by Burma/Myanmar, Thailand had
experienced a military coup. Migrant organisations and the workers themselves had deep reservations about the necessity to return
to their homes in order to obtain identity and travel documents.
There were widespread reports that the Burmese authorities were
conducting house inspections, seeking details of absent household members and requiring families to hang outside their house
photographs of all family members to enable them to check who
had migrated;[34] this created the fear that family members might
be punished or forced to pay taxes or other charges if migrants
signed up to the new process.

According to figures published on the MAP Foundation website,
as of 12 May 2010 there were some 1.3 million migrants in Thailand
eligible for nationality verification, of whom 82 per cent were
Burmese. Of these, fewer than 210,000 had actually completed
the process. Although the vast majority of eligible migrants were
from Burma, they represented only 35 per cent of those who had
actually obtained their documents. This is partly because the
Laotians and Cambodians initiated the process much earlier, but
also because the Thai government assured Burmese migrants who
signalled their intention to enter the process that they were safe
from deportation until their application was completed. The whole
procedure is fraught with obstacles since it requires attendance at
specific offices, submitting a range of documents that few migrants
have in their possession, and paying a series of fees. Because of
the complicated procedure and document requirements, many have
been forced to use Thai or Burmese agents, who extort very high
payment for their services, which adds to the costs involved in

paying the official fees of up to 4,000 baht required to obtain the passport and the work permit.[35] In May 2011 the Thai government was offering a 'last chance' to undocumented migrants to register and obtain the relevant documents, promising a crackdown on those caught without permission to work in the country.

Given the focus on the mechanisms for registration of illegal migrant workers in Thailand, it might be assumed that obtaining official documents and achieving registered status would protect them from harassment by the authorities and ensure that they would receive their legal entitlement in terms of minimum wage and appropriate social protection, and that they would not have to suffer exploitation and deprivation in their place of employment.

Indeed, as noted above, Thai employers have put intense pressure on the government to regulate migrant workers in order to facilitate the employment of cheap labour in their factories and other workplaces. But the actual situation is far more complex. As we detail in Chapter 4, even under the old system of registration migrant factory workers who had obtained documents were not protected, not least because the documentation is routinely held by the employers. The new system, which allows workers to change employer under specific circumstances, has added to the incentive for employers to retain the documents – in order to minimize the risk of workers shifting to competitors. It is widely reported that neither the police nor the immigration authorities will accept photo-copies as official proof of registration, and instead demand 'fines' and bribes from migrant workers. Although the temporary passport is valid for five years, work permits are only valid for two years, subject to a single renewal. This involves high costs for the workers, who, particularly in the current climate, cannot be certain that their employment will continue or that they will not be arbitrarily deported from the country; hence the investment of money and time is very risky. The relatively small number of Burmese migrant workers who have obtained the temporary passports generally work in the larger and more formal establishments, and have received help from their employers, who are willing to operate within the law, usually in the form of the employer paying the upfront fees and deducting the costs from the workers' wages (which is a further incentive for the employer to retain the documentation). For others, including garment workers employed in smaller workshops of so-called 'house factories', as well as the armies of construction, agricultural and fishing workers, and domestic workers confined physically to their employers' households, there is little prospect of such assistance and protection. With the cost of registration running to the equivalent of a whole month's earnings or more, registration is out of their reach. Unless migrant workers have had a substantial period of employment in Thailand and can count on a stable income over time, they are not able to meet the registration costs independently. Some enterprising migrants have been known to hire a Thai 'employer' and obtain independent registration. However, given the escalating costs of the newly introduced passport system, and the frequent changes in rules and procedures, as well as the restricted time limits on applying for and completing the process, it has become very difficult for migrants to register without the backing of a specific employer.

The system is in fact stacked in favour of the employer. Whilst migrant workers are in theory able to change employer, the practice is far from straightforward. When workers want to change employer, they need a written agreement from the former employer to release them and one from the new employer to re-register them; this makes a change virtually impossible. It is not surprising, therefore, that in spite of efforts to crack down on illegal migrant workers in Thailand by enhanced cooperation with sending countries, the number of unregistered migrant workers continues to grow. In terms of the employment of migrants in the export-oriented manufactures sector, which is the focus of this book, employing undocumented workers continues to be an attractive option, not least for small operations that seek to undercut competitors by reducing labour and operating costs, rather than increasing productivity. Registration adds to the cost of employing migrant workers, as well as to the management necessary to organise them.

Unregistered workers, on the other hand, are bound to employers out of fear of discovery and deportation, making them even more vulnerable to a regime of long working hours, wage deductions, and confinement in often substandard accommodation in factory compounds or, in the case of 'house factories', within the factory itself. In the name of protecting workers from the attentions of the police and immigration authorities – adding to the fear of a strange place, an alien language and hostility from the local population – employers are frequently able to confine their workers physically to the factories, where they are able to control their lives as well as their labour.

The new system of migrant worker registration has been devised in a context in which the Thai government faces many different pressures and policy drivers. The MOUs on registration of migrant labour have been enacted partly as the result of international pressure concerning agreements on human trafficking and drug smuggling, but also in the context of renewed emphasis on Thailand's relations with its neighbours and its position within ASEAN and the region. At the same time the government faces a domestic constituency in which industrialists continue to press for access to cheap migrant labour, while official and popular concern grows regarding the threat of migrants to Thailand's border and internal security.

Migrant workers and the Thai economy

There is a widely held view within Thailand that 'alien' workers bring little or no benefit to the economy. In spite of recent efforts to introduce a more rational policy for the control of migrant workers, there are repeated calls for limiting the employment of migrants, for restricting them to specified residential zones, and for prioritising employment of Thai workers in the name of national security.

This view was disputed by a 2007 ILO study, which details the high monetary contribution of migrant workers, in terms of social security and health insurance payments for services that few use; their contribution to maintaining export and foreign exchange earnings; the ways in which they fill labour shortages and provide flexibility for Thai businesses; and their part in improving efficiency and productivity in key economic sectors.

Nevertheless, many people still believe that the presence of migrant workers needs to be tightly controlled to prevent them from threatening the employment and well-being of Thai citizens. There are fears that migrant workers exert a downward pressure on wages, because they weaken the negotiating power of trade unions and prevent the labour shortages which lead to rises in income. But the significant gap between the earnings of migrant workers and their Thai counterparts suggests that it is the migrants themselves who feel the effects of low wages, protecting the average wage levels of Thai workers.[36] Moreover, it is clear that Thai workers do not compete for the same jobs as migrant workers, who are concentrated in labour-intensive and marginal occupations, dubbed 3D jobs (see Chapter 1).

Public opinion in Thailand remains unsympathetic to the presence of migrant workers from Burma and elsewhere. A police officer interviewed in the *Bangkok Post* on 26 June 2007 considered that having migrant children studying in the town centre led to potential security problems:

> For safety, the migrant population should be in a restricted zone under state control. Also, if they want to study, their older peers should do the teaching, not our people. I cannot see how educating these children can benefit our country in any way. We have to think about the burden society must shoulder if these children decide to stay on.

Although official policy is to provide all children in the country with basic education (see Chapter 5), access to education for migrant children in Thailand is restricted, regardless of their tax and other contributions. Furthermore, although many registered migrant workers enjoy a degree of access to Thai public health services, they tend to make limited use of them. Negative public attitudes and even hostility towards migrant workers persist. Large numbers of migrant workers, both women and men, continue to be arrested, detained and deported, as we discuss in Chapter 4. Since the 2008 crisis, migrant workers in Mae Sot and other places have become the target of both official and vigilante violence. In central provinces of Thailand, such as Samut Sakorn, there are reports of Thai gangs roaming the streets and harassing Burmese migrants, especially during night-time,[37] reflecting fears expressed by local people that their town – and their economic futures – were being taken over by the migrants. In a situation of widespread economic and political insecurity, it is no surprise that foreign migrant workers are once again being blamed.[38]

In terms of poverty reduction, Thailand is recognised as one of the stars of the twentieth century, reducing rural poverty from above 60 per cent in the early 1960s to less than 10 per cent in the new century.[39] Yet the country's transformation into an economy based on the production and export of manufacturing and services often overlooks the role played by exploited migrant workers. The rise in Thai wages – one of the consequences of the economic progress seen in the last four decades of the twentieth century – was the reason factories started to look for cheaper labour outside Bangkok, both in remote parts of the country and beyond. The two most recent economic crises in Thailand, in 1997 and in 2008/9, witnessed what would appear to be a contradiction: many Thai workers lost their jobs as external and internal demand for Thai manufactures fell sharply; at the same time enterprises increased their demand for 'cheap' labour, which was met by the hiring of migrants – mainly Burmese, and in particular young women. These often unacknowledged, unseen and unregistered workers thus became an indispensable source of economic growth for Thailand, providing a supply of cheap and flexible labour for the export industries. The Thai government, with the support of industrialists, has introduced a series of registration schemes for migrant workers, which keep them designated 'alien' and illegal, but allow them to be employed temporarily. Thus migrant workers have become the ultimate flexible labour force in Thailand. In the following chapters, we show how such labour migration policies have shaped the lives and perspectives of Burmese women and men migrant workers.

3

Burmese women migrant workers in Thailand's export industries

Burmese migrant workers in Thailand come from every corner of Burma, seeking to escape political and economic difficulties and to find opportunities to work and earn money in the more prosperous neighbouring country of Thailand. Their journey to Thailand is not just a physical one involving crossing the border and finding a place where they can live and work. It is also a personal journey, which reflects and shapes their relations with families and friends, and their perceptions of themselves and their country. Most of the Burmese women and men we encountered had embarked on their migratory journey when they were quite young – in their late teens and early twenties. The journey to Thailand and their experiences in seeking employment and living and working in the factories involve a number of struggles: to find work, to organise accommodation, to survive and to attain an acceptable level of security in an often hostile and difficult environment, and in time to access health and education services for themselves and their families. In the course of this journey, their identities are shaped by their encounters with their employers, their fellow workers, the local population and representatives of the Thai state, all of which sharpen their perception of their own (lack of) entitlements and

citizenship in both home and destination countries. This chapter
explores the multidimensional nature of the journeys undertaken
by Burmese migrant workers who have left their homes in Burma
to work in Thailand's manufacturing factories.[1]

The number of migrant workers in Thailand today is estimated
at between 1.5 and 3 million, with 80 per cent coming from Burma,
the rest from Laos and Cambodia. They are spread across various
occupations, including construction, fisheries and seafood processing, agriculture, rice mills, light manufacturing and domestic
work, all of which come into the category of low-paid 3D sectors
where it has proved more difficult to recruit Thai labour. There are
particular concentrations of migrant workers in the fishing port of
Mahachai near Bangkok and in Ranong in the South in fish-related
industries, with men working on the boats and in portering, and
women (often with the help of their children) employed in the
processes of cleaning and peeling shrimps and prawns. Agriculture
and construction employ both male and female workers, with a
slight balance towards men. An estimated 300,000 – or 40 per
cent of the total – domestic workers in Thailand are migrant
women, mostly employed on a live-in basis, carrying out child
and other family care as well as cleaning and domestic work.
Migrant workers are also employed in restaurants and informal
food outlets, in entertainment and sex work, in filling stations, and
in markets. These are all jobs that demand long working hours,
and are insecure and badly paid.[2]

Some 20 per cent of migrants, mostly those working in domestic, construction and service work, are in Bangkok, with a
large majority of the remaining migrant population concentrated
in the central, north and south regions close to the border with
Burma, where fishing and fish-processing industries and other
export-based industries are located. In the garment and textile
export factories in the border areas, which mushroomed after the
1997 crisis, some 80 per cent of the workers are young women, who
reflect the model of the ideal worker in export factories – young,
female and docile. The manufacturing factories, which are major

employers of Burmese migrant workers, are mainly concentrated in the central provinces around Bangkok, and increasingly in towns close to the Burmese border. Our research was carried out in three locations where there are concentrations of garment and textile factories employing Burmese migrant workers: (i) Mae Sot district in Tak province, in the western part of Thailand at the border with Burma; (ii) Three Pagodas Pass, in Sangklaburi district of Kanchanaburi province, in the western part of Thailand, which is adjacent to the Burmese border; (iii) an area in the centre of the country that includes Prapadaeng district of Samut Prakan province and Bang Kunthien district of Bangkok. These are long-standing locations for garment production in Thailand, for both export and domestic markets, and all have experienced a rise in the employment of migrant workers in recent years.

   After the financial crisis of 1997 the fastest growth in factories employing migrant workers was in Mae Sot; the more central areas nearer to Bangkok experienced a labour shortage from around 2002, as the economy recovered; while the expansion in Three Pagodas Pass is more recent, dating from about 2006. Export markets include not only the USA, Europe and Japan but also China and neighbouring countries.

The study areas

Mae Sot

According to the labour office of Tak Province, the 1997 economic crisis in Thailand provided opportunities for Tak Province because as a border province with Burma it can access large quantities of cheap labour, which has made it an attractive destination for labour-intensive industries considering relocation to reduce costs and take advantage of government decentralisation policies. Figure 3.1 indicates the growth of garment factories since they began to locate in Mae Sot in the early 1990s.

   The first factory in Mae Sot began production in 1991; the following decade saw a dramatic increase in the number of both workers

FIGURE 3.1   Apparel factories and workers in Tak province

workers   factories

Source Thai National Office of Statistics website.

and factories. The first half of the decade witnessed a fast rate of growth as industrialists responded to increasing international market competition as well as the incentives offered for firms to relocate to the border areas; since the end of the 1990s, following the difficulties experienced due to the financial crisis, the rate of relocation accelerated. Recent data indicate that this growth has continued, though there was a slowdown in 2008/9 as Thailand absorbed the shocks of the global financial crisis of 2007/8.

Consequently, Mae Sot has one of the highest concentrations of migrant workers from Burma. In 2004, there were over 120,000 Burmese workers registered in Tak province, accounting for over 13 per cent of the total number registered in Thailand,[3] although the actual numbers, including non-registered migrants, was likely to have been double that number.[4] However, the number of migrants in Mae Sot who have registered under the new nationality verification process is reportedly quite low, as employers are able to take advantage of the close proximity to the border, avoiding the cost and trouble of registration since the workers can always flee to the Burmese side of the river in the event of a police raid, as in the incident in 2007 described in Chapter 1. But this situation may well be changing, given the new economic and political crises in the region. Between 8 and 10 May 2010 factories in Mae Sot were raided by the police, and over 600 undocumented workers were arrested.[5] Nevertheless, there is every indication that the instability of the garment sector combined with the ease of crossing between countries in Mae Sot – not just the official 'Friendship Bridge' but also large stretches of the Moei river – make this one of the most porous borders between Thailand and Burma. Migrant workers in the Mae Sot factories number not just those from the Karen provinces close to the border but include many from Burma's interior provinces, since the road links between Mae Sot and large population centres such as Yangon (Rangoon)[6] are very good.

Some 80 per cent of the workers we interviewed in Mae Sot initially migrated as teenagers, with members of their family or community joining them as time went on. Many women reported that they were forced to give up their jobs and return home when they got married and had children, though we met a significant number who have remained in or returned to Mae Sot once they had a family, with some women and men claiming up to eight or ten years' experience in the factories.

There are a variety of different types of factory in and around Mae Sot, ranging from large, modern-looking structures that employ more than a thousand workers (though not all on the same shift) to smaller-scale factories with a few hundred workers, down to the so-called 'house factories' employing up to fifty workers. The most visible are the large establishments on the outskirts of town – modular structures built fairly recently with modern materials. On our first visit to this location in 2004 we were struck by the anonymity of these factories. None of them displayed the normal identifiers seen on factories around the world, such as the name of the manufacturer or subcontractor, phone or other contact details of the management, information about vacancies, and so forth. Indeed the first thing visitors were likely to see was surly security guards at the gate – both Thai and Burmese – though it was not clear if the purpose was to keep intruders out or the workers inside. These large factories are generally owned and managed by Thai industrialists, working on contracts for major contractors in Bangkok, or directly for foreign global brands – such as Tommy Hilfiger, Top Form International and Absorba (a global maternity and infant clothing brand). Some of the factories are owned by investors from Taiwan and Hong Kong, though foreign companies operating in Thailand require Thai business partners.

The smaller-scale factories are located upriver from the centre of the town (where the bridge linking Myawaddy and Mae Sot is located). These are more modest, even ramshackle, structures, crowded fairly close together in an area lacking metalled roads, and with relatively poor sanitary and other infrastructure. Both types of factory generally have 'dormitories' attached, most of which are purpose-built concrete cells – reminiscent more of workers' housing in tea plantations in Sri Lanka than of the smarter modern accommodation constructed in the 1990s in Thailand's Northern Region Industrial Estate (NRIE) to house the Thai workers employed in the electronics factories there.[7] Workers with families rent accommodation in the dilapidated houses around the factories.

However, the migrants working in the 'house factories' do not have separate accommodation supplied by their employer. These are workshops established within the homes of Thai entrepreneurs, who have converted or extended their houses to accommodate sewing machines, crowding the workers into multiple occupancy dorms or even requiring them to sleep in the same rooms as they work, though over the years many workers have found lodgings outside the factories, living with friends, relatives or families. The work regime in these workshops is much more intensive, requiring the women to be at their machine from 6 a.m. until 9 p.m., with only short breaks for meals. These women, so far as we could tell, were virtually lacking documents, and often had relied on agents linked to the owners to place them in employment; hence they remained in debt for a long period of time. Some said they did not go out to the town because they did not speak Thai and were afraid of being arrested or questioned by police. The only time they did leave the factory was on their monthly day off to buy supplies and to remit what money they could save to their families back in Burma.

Workers in 'house factories' often receive lower pay than those employed in the larger factories, and frequently complain about irregular payment. Those we spoke to told us that they continued to work in these establishments because they had been unable to secure employment in the larger and better-paying factories, or because they had been able to find accommodation nearby, and did not want to travel far due to the cost of transportation and a desire to elude policy vigilance. Many of these workers were either very young recent migrants or older women who had migrated when they were already parents, and had strong obligations to their families at home.

Sangklaburi (Three Pagodas Pass)

Three Pagodas Pass is located at the border between Sangklaburi district, Thailand, and Karen State, Burma. The towns on both sides of the border are called Three Pagodas Pass – *Payathonzu* in Burmese and *Phra Chedi Sam Ong* in Thai. Until 2007, this place flourished as a tourist destination, but conflict between Thai and Burmese soldiers forced the closure of the border gate. However, local people continued to use the small informal crossings along the border without hindrance. While the economy on the Burmese side has deteriorated as a result of the reduction in tourism, the availability of cheap, willing labour has stimulated the establishment of a range of factories manufacturing footwear, garments and mosquito nets on the Thai side. The first garment factory was established in 1996. The footwear factory, the largest employer in the area, which produces for an international brand name for export, was established in 2006. In 2008 there were around eighty factories in Three Pagodas Pass employing around 3,300 workers.[8] All employ Burmese labour. The legal status of Three Pagodas Pass is somewhat complex. Although it is a militarized zone, it has also been established as a Free Trade Zone. It would appear that the local authorities on both side of the border have an agreement to allow Burmese workers to commute daily and without hindrance to work on the Thai side, although they are not permitted to stay overnight. Therefore many workers actually live on the Burmese side of the border, where the cost of living is lower, and commute daily to the factories on the Thai side to work. In the absence of surveillance and control by the police and immigration authorities, there is little tension in the town.

Officially both Mae Sot and Three Pagodas Pass have a lower minimum wage rate than Samut Prakhan; but since most workers in Three Pagodas Pass work solely on a piece-rate basis, they earn much less even than those in Mae Sot, and as a consequence many workers seek to relocate to other parts of Thailand where they can earn more.

Most of the workplaces in Three Pagodas Pass are small house factories employing fewer than thirty workers. They normally have one big working room, which is packed with sewing machines, knitting machines and a cutting section, as well as quality control and packing. The largest employer, the footwear factory, has around 1,000 workers in all, divided between three establishments, since no single building is large enough to accommodate all the workers. The factory is popular among the migrant workers, as the pay is better and regular. There is always a long line of hopeful Burmese migrants in front of the factory waiting for vacancies to be announced.

There are some 200 small factories in Three Pagodas Pass, all manufacturing garments except for about a dozen which make footwear and miscellaneous textile products. The factories are generally subcontracted from firms in Bangkok, including several which sew mosquito nets for the United Nations anti-malaria campaigns. Most are linked to small or medium-sized enterprises in Bangkok, which often send partially finished garments by bus to Three Pagodas Pass for further sewing. The vast majority of the factories in this area are owned by Thais, though there are also a few small house factories managed by Burmese entrepreneurs, who rent houses from local Thai nationals, since they are not legally entitled to own property in Thailand.

Phrapradaeng district, Samut Prakan[9]

Samut Prakan is a province adjacent to Bangkok, and one of the most industrialised provinces in Thailand. This has been a long-standing location for the production of garments, textiles and other products, mainly employing Thai workers, though, as indicated above, there has been a growth in the hiring of migrant workers, mainly Burmese, in the last decade. At the time of our research Burmese[10] made up around 15 per cent of the total employment in registered establishments in the province.[11] This area was especially hard hit by the 2008 economic crisis; Ministry of Labour figures show that the number of workers laid off in Samut Prakan was the second highest in the country (the highest being Pathumthani province, north of Bangkok) in 2008.[12]

Unlike at the other research sites, a number of larger export-oriented factories in Samut Prakan require the Burmese workers they employ to be registered. Those unable to obtain registration documents find work in small workshops, where working conditions and pay are inferior – generally below the minimum wage level for the location. In some factories, particularly in central Thailand, Burmese workers work alongside Thai workers and, in theory, are paid the same wage. However, we found that many factories, particularly those that employ a large number of migrant workers, organise their workforce along ethnic lines, so they are able to pay lower wages to Burmese workers, who rarely work alongside Thai workers in production. Even when the wage is the same, it would appear that Burmese workers, who are by definition temporary, do not receive the same non-wage benefits as the Thais, such as provision of work uniforms and child allowances. However, migrant workers in Samut Prakan reported that they were able to earn higher wages than those prevailing in the other two research areas. The average pay in Samut Prakhan, based on the minimum wage for the area at the time of our research in 2008, was 203 baht per day; in Mae Sot, where the official minimum wage is lower, workers reported that they are entitled to a daily rate of approximately 150 baht per day, but that after deductions they are lucky if they receive 60 baht.

Some 41 per cent of registered migrant workers in Samut Prakan were women, a lower proportion than in other locations, reflecting the fact that there are a number of more capital-intensive textile and garment factories, as well as several making leather goods and footwear, which tend to hire more men.[13] Because Burmese migrant workers are in the minority in this location, they are under more pressure to assimilate to Thai society; in contrast to Mae Sot, the town does not feel like a Burmese outpost. Migrant workers in Samut Prakan were dressed exactly like Thais; most of the women we observed attending the weekend schools that offered Thai and English language classes were dressed in white shirts and black skirts, and were indistinguishable from Thai university students of the same age. The women told us that the schools themselves requested that they dressed in this way in order to gain respect from the Thai people who lived nearby. It would seem that many migrant workers were keen to demonstrate their desire to fit in with their host society, not just in terms of how they dressed but in other ways too, such as decorating their houses with photographs of the Thai king. When we asked them to explain why they did this, the reply was: 'We are living in his country and we want to show respect.'

In Three Pagodas Pass there is as yet no question of migrant workers assimilating to Thai patterns of dress or cultural habit since in the main workers make a daily journey across the border to work; as in Mae Sot, the only Thais in the factories are supervisors and managers.

In the central areas, however, migrant workers have attempted to adapt and integrate into the host society, reflecting the journey they have made; their behaviour reveals their preference to remain in Thailand and access whatever opportunities are available in terms of employment and stability for themselves and their families.

Migrant women's journeys

Migrant workers leave their villages and their people to seek new opportunities in Thailand. As well as physical relocation, migration also involves psychological and social changes related to being in new situations, meeting new people and to the stresses and successes inherent in surviving and adapting to such changes. Whilst many accounts of migrant workers in different parts of the world focus exclusively on the economic and structural factors that determine decisions to migrate, here we draw on the voices of Burmese migrant women in Thailand who relate the contradictions and complexities of their migratory experiences.

Leaving home

It is not always the case that the women and men who go to Thailand to seek work are from the poorest or the most deprived or the most marginalised groups in Burma, since migrants everywhere require human and financial resources that are generally beyond the reach of the 'poorest of the poor'. But the Burmese migrant workers to whom we spoke indicated that the common catalyst behind their decision to leave home was the lack of opportunity in Burma – not just for day-to-day survival but in terms of creating a better future for themselves. Although migrant workers are from a range of ethnic groups, the majority in our survey (69.8 per cent) were from the dominant ethnic group, Burman, with most of the remaining being Karen (12.5 per cent) and Mon (11.9 per cent), with a small number from the Shan, Rakhaing, Pa-O and Dawai ethnic groups. The largest number in our survey came from Mon State (31 per cent), one of the border states adjacent to Thailand, but a substantial proportion were from Pegu division (21 per cent) and Yangon division (19 per cent), which are in the centre of the country. This indicates that migrant workers in Thailand do not necessarily originate from the areas in closest proximity to the factories. Rather, they follow migratory paths of family and others from their place of origin; hence it is common to find concentrations of workers from a particular location in specific factories. Most of the migrant workers in the factories are relatively well educated. On average, women respondents had 7.6 years of schooling, the men 8.6 years; 13 women respondents (out of 371) and 6 men respondents (out of 133) had gone on to tertiary education, reflecting the fact that their backgrounds were often urban, and that previously their families had been relatively prosperous. Although migrants are not from the most marginalised section of Burmese society, there were wide reports of families left behind experiencing economic difficulties. Many households were in debt because families had to borrow money from neighbours or money lenders in order to pay the exorbitant taxes levied by the Burmese authorities, which was a major catalyst for many women who had come to Thailand to seek waged work. Some women claimed that their houses in Yangon had been burnt down and they had been forcibly removed to a satellite town, where there was no possibility of finding work. [14] One of our respondents, Tin Moe Aung, a single Burman woman in her early thirties who came to Thailand in 2004 to work in Three Pagodas Pass, recalled that she had sought employment in a garment factory in Yangon because repeated flooding had made it impossible for her family to continue to maintain themselves from farming:

> I have five siblings and I am the youngest. My oldest brother and third brother are married and have their own families in Yangon and in our hometown [Ayeyawady division]. They have their own businesses but [there is only] just enough for their families. They can't support my parents. One of my older sisters, who is single, supports our parents. Another older sister is married and works on our parents' farm... In 1999, I came to Yangon to seek a better job

because farming is difficult and produced very little profit because our hometown gets flooded every year. So our family experienced a very difficult financial situation... [when I came to Yangon] I stayed with my aunt and brother and worked in the factories. In 2001, I got a job in a garment factory in Yangon after learning how to sew... Later, the supervisor in the factory allowed me to stay rent-free, which was better than living with my aunt because her house was crowded and she always needed money for her family... I earned 40,000 kyat a month and then I could remit to my parents.

However, pay in the garment factories in Yangon was very low and the working hours were very long. Thanda Hlaing, a Burman women in her mid-thirties with a university degree, now living and working in Three Pagodas Pass, told us that when she was working in Yangon she had to get up at 5 a.m. to catch the bus to go to factory and only returned at 10 p.m. Her working hours are still very long in Thailand, but she says she is better off than at home because she does not waste time commuting, and cooking and other housework are much easier and quicker in Thailand because gas and other facilities are available.

At least three-quarters of the women with whom we conducted in-depth interviews related that they had migrated out of a sense of duty to their parents, even if they were initially reluctant to leave their homes. Mu Mu Han is a 20-year-old single Burman woman from Yangon, who migrated to Three Pagodas Pass in 2010. Her testimony demonstrates that migration is often a family decision fuelled by complex motivations:

After I finished grade 10, I did not want [to continue study], so I worked in a tea leaves factory for 2 years. Then I learned motor sewing [using an industrial sewing machine] from my aunt, who uses [the machine] at her house. Then I applied for jobs in several garment factories. I moved from one factory to another but when I got a job in the Daewoo garment factory, I liked the job and worked there for three years. In the home-based factories where I worked at first I earned only 30,000 kyats [1,000 Thai baht] a month; in Daewoo I earned 70,000 kyats [2,300 Thai baht] a month. In addition, I was paid a bonus of 20,000 k [660 Thai baht] every

Thingyan (New Year) festival. When we worked the whole night,
I earned 3,000 k [100 baht] a night. If we worked on a holiday we
got extra 2000 k [66 baht]... We had holidays every Saturday and
Sunday. On those days I went downtown with my friends... In the
morning my mother cooked for me; she cooked very good curries
for me every morning... She likes cleaning, so at home the kitchen
is always clean and all the pots are bright and shining all the time...
She never spends money carelessly. From the money I gave her, she
bought a gold ring and a necklace for me [as savings]... [Coming
here to Thailand] is my mother's wish. My mother has a friend in
the market whose sons work in Three Pagodas Pass. They came back
home once a year and told my mother that there are better working
opportunities and wages in Three Pagodas Pass, so she urged me to
come here, although I didn't want to leave as I was happy working in
the Daewoo factory with my friends... Because of my mother, I came
here. She said if I earn more I can use my savings to set up a business in the future, and that will make my life more stable... Also, my
mother didn't like my boyfriend so she sent me here to separate me
from him... in the end I agreed to come, thinking that I would gain
experience and knowledge by working in other parts of the country,
at the border. (Mu Mu Han of Three Pagodas Pass)

Others were more enthusiastic about finding work in Thailand
in order to support their parents. May Thin Aye, a Burman woman
in her late twenties from Yangon, came to Thailand in 2004, got
married and had children.

I was working in a garment factory in Yangon. I can sew skilfully. I
heard that there was an opportunity to come and work in Mae Sot
from my neighbours who work in Mae Sot and remit 100,000 k per
month back home. I was impressed and I decided to come to work in
Mae Sot with the aim of remitting to my parents. I discussed it with
my two older sisters, who were working in the same garment factory
in Yangon. We asked for permission from our parents to come
and they arranged for us to come with my aunt, whose daughter is
working in Mae Sot. (May Thin Aye in Mae Sot)

Some have obligations to support their younger siblings, which
they prioritise, often over their own futures. Tin Nwe Soe, a
Burman woman working in Mae Sot, left university before graduat-
ing and came to Thailand in 2004 to work.

I have responsibility for my youngest brother, who is very keen to finish his university education... If I get married now, I couldn't support my brother, who needs money for his university education. I want to support him by working with my other two older sisters. My earnings alone are not sufficient for him and my two older sisters' earnings alone are not sufficient either. We have to combine all three earnings to be able to pay for my brother's university fees and my mother's house/food expenses. I will think about marriage after my brother finishes university, maybe in the next three years.

However, the journey to Thailand is not easy. Thet Htar Lwin recalled how her sister came to Thailand to work for the sake of the family, but was cheated by a friend.

[My sister] felt sorry for the family. She is the oldest and has a sense of responsibility towards the family. She felt the family couldn't improve their life if she continued to work in the town. She worked in the shop with me [in Yangon]. When she came with her friend to Bangkok to work for a construction firm, they had debt to the agent who got them the jobs. After one month, her friend fled back to Burma without telling the boss, leaving my sister responsible for the debt owed by both of them. She had to work for the boss without being paid for a whole year to pay off the debt... After working for two years, she got married to a man she met at work, but exactly one year later her husband was killed in front of her eyes when he fell off a building on which he was working.

In common with many young women who work in factories all around the world, some workers are motivated by their desire to 'see the world' as well as 'stand on their own feet'. Hnin Cho is a Burman woman in her mid-twenties with a 6th grade education, who is now working in Samut Prakan. Even though her parents are well off and do not need financial help, she insists that she came to work in Thailand in order to be independent from her family: 'My siblings are working for themselves. We like to work and earn money for ourselves rather than being dependent on each other.'

May Thu Maw, another Burman woman from Yangon in her late thirties, recalled that her decision to work in the border factories in Three Pagodas Pass, was made in the face of family opposition.

> I worked for twelve years in Yangon in the garment factory. I have sewed since I was 15 years old. But my earnings were too low. I earned 15,000 kyat a month but many of the workers in my factory went to Three Pagodas Pass and got a good income so they could send remittances home... That is why I decided to come here. I discussed it with my parents and siblings, who are all government employees, and they did not agree with me. Finally I convinced my mother to let me leave home because I wanted to go so badly.

Wives as well as daughters see working in the border factories as a route to independence and new experiences:

> The reason I came here is because I quarrelled with my husband and left the house... I also wanted to earn my own money so that I can use it as I want. I wanted to develop more knowledge by coming to the border area. (Nandar Cho of Three Pagodas Pass)

Others come with their husbands in order to earn money to support their children, and to contribute towards a better future, even if this creates difficulties within the family:

> [My husband wanted to go back to] his previous job [in Yangon], but the garage [that he used to work in] was sold and there was no longer a job for him, so we could not stay in Yangon. Immediately [after he lost his job], we both arranged to come to Thailand, because we needed to pay the expenses and school fees for our two children. We came to Mae Sot to work. I wanted my husband to work in construction sites here, where he could earn 150 baht a day, but he was keen on going to Bangkok because he had worked there before. He thinks the wages in Mae Sot are too low... My sister, who is here, didn't want to go to Bangkok either, because we needed to pay 17,000 baht each for the agent's fees to take us there. Since we did not have the money, we had to borrow it and had to get into debt... If something happens to my children [while I am in Bangkok] I would have to go back to Yangon. In that case, our investment in the form of the agent's fee to go to Bangkok would be lost. Then I thought

very carefully and decided to work in a factory [in Mae Sot]... I often think of quitting the job [because it is tiring to stand the whole day], but when I think about my children and our wish to build a house so that we can stay together, I overcome my stress and now... I am happy to work. But I still miss my children. (Kaythi Min Soe of Mae Sot)

More and more young people in Burma have been keen to come to Thailand to work as the information about job opportunities and connections to those already working in Thailand have grown over the years. Even when parents have been reluctant to allow their daughters to migrate, they often overcome their misgivings if the young woman is able to join relatives and friends already in Thailand. In Mae Sot, in particular, there is a dense network of Burmese migrants, which makes parents feel more relaxed about young girls leaving home, though they are often more worried about those who travel to Bangkok or further afield. The lack of opportunities in Burma, coupled with better economic prospects for employment in Thailand, is changing the way parents see their daughters, and many are now encouraging them to migrate. However, some Burmese parents have come to regret such encouragement, as increasing numbers of young Burmese women are getting married and having children in Thailand, and do not appear to want to return home. As we discuss in Chapter 5, in the face of ongoing economic and political difficulties, many Burmese parents are now following their children to Thailand, seeking to rebuild their family away from their home and their country.

Crossing the border

Leaving familiar social networks behind, migrant workers venture into a new world; dreaming of becoming rich and returning home in triumph, they take with them high hopes and ambitions, and a commitment to their families back home, but they soon realise that the journey to Thailand presents unforeseen challenges as well as opportunities. Coming from an isolated and nominally socialist planned economy, they encounter new forms of state and market that they have never experienced before, and meet different people who can change the course of their lives forever.

The first challenge that migrant workers face is the physical journey from their home town to the border and beyond. For some, the journey is easy and straightforward; for others it is extremely uncomfortable; and for the unfortunate few the experience feels as though they are the subject of trafficking. Most migrants had heard about working in Thailand from their neighbours and friends, and had a ready-made network to assist them; others were encouraged by their parents, who had learned of the experience of other families whose children had migrated. In all cases the workers had needed help from others – preferably relatives, friends or neighbours, but often an agent specialised in organising the illegal entry to Thailand and, in many cases, introducing them to their first employer. Whatever the migratory route, there were considerable costs involved: travel to a border area of Burma, the crossing of a river or land border, paying for accommodation in the place of destination, and paying the agent for organising the trip and finding them a job.

According to our survey, in 2008 agents charged an average fee of 200 baht for the journey to Mae Sot, 716 baht to Three Pagodas Pass, and a massive 13,800 baht to reach Bangkok. In addition, migrants had to pay 35 baht to cross the border at the official gate, but if they needed to use an unofficial crossing, then the cost was 700 baht. Moreover, they often incurred further costs during the time they were waiting to start work.

The migrants reported that the journey inside Burma to get to the border was arduous. Some took days to reach the border, because roads and transportation in Burma are quite bad, and they had to spend nights en route in curry shops, which offer temporary accommodation. Accidents on the journey were frequent since many vehicles were not adequate for the road conditions and the number of passengers they had to carry. This was the first time many of them had travelled away from their homes, which can be very stressful. However, even if, as in the case of

Nandar Cho, a young woman from Yangon with three children and a heavy-drinking husband, the journey to Thailand offered an opportunity to explore a new world, at the same time it presented many challenges:

> When I was in Mu Don Hotel I felt very lonely staying alone in the room. I have never had such an experience. At the time, I thought several times of turning back and going home, but then I thought 'Oh I will not go back since I have left home, I will go until I arrive at my destination.' But during the three-day trip I frequently thought 'I am wrong to come on this trip' but I didn't want to give up so I continued. Then when I arrived here [Three Pagodas Pass], I met my friends and the factory manager's wife from my village helped me with everything I needed. So now I am happy.

Tin Moe Aung, a Burman woman in her early thirties from Yangon, told us about her hazardous and costly journey to Three Pagodas Pass:

> While I was working in the garment factory in Yangon, my brother's wife's sister told me about better job opportunities in Three Pagodas Pass. She had a friend who is an agent ... The agent told us that we didn't have to bring anything – except some clothes to wear, and money to buy food on the way, and she would provide all the transportation fees and the cost would be deducted from the wages we would earn in the future. We were six women and four men, who went together. It took 5 days to get to Three Pagodas Pass because the car broke down on the way. When we got to the border we were sent to work at a [garment] factory on the Burmese side. Although we worked there for 45 days we didn't get paid, so we tried to escape. With the help of the woman we were renting a room from we were able to contact the leader of the village. One day when we were allowed to go out, we went out and reported our situation to the police, who sent us to the township office to make a complaint.

Even after she succeeded in crossing to Thailand, Tin Moe Aung encountered further bad luck; when she tried to travel further inland, anti-government demonstrations prevented her from reaching Bangkok.

My sister and I decided travel to Bangkok through an agent. At that time there was a big [red shirt] protest in Bangkok. On the way we were kept in a house for fifteen days, and during that time we spent all our money... The agent told us to wait until the situation in Bangkok had become calm. We felt embarrassed about going back to Three Pagodas Pass because all our friends knew that we had left for Bangkok. I even thought of going back to Burma and to become a nun for life [because I was feeling so ashamed]. In the end, we asked the agent to bring us back to Three Pagodas Pass.

Zin Min Swe, who came to Thailand in her mid-twenties, was also misled. Not only was her journey hazardous and costly, but she was also the victim of misinformation from migrants already in Thailand. The desire not to lose face with family and friends at home propels many migrant workers to hide the difficulties and disappointments of their work and life, fuelling false expectations in those influenced by their narratives, who are also trapped by the investment in the migratory journey and the importance of maintaining 'face'.

Oh, it was a terrible trip... I was working in a garment factory in Yangon... At first, I was not interested in coming... One girl from the first group of people who went [to Three Pagodas Pass] wrote a letter to her mother, saying that she was well and that her job was good, and she remitted some money to her mother. Her mother encouraged us to go to Three Pagodas Pass – saying there were no reasons to be afraid. So my friends and I decided to come as well... There were thirty of us, only one was a boy. [We travelled by train, van, then walked, and took a boat.] The agents had hired a truck to bring us to Three Pagodas Pass... All thirty people were squashed at the back, with no space to sit, and we just stood without anything to hold on to... The factory was on the Burmese side. We didn't even know that Three Pagodas Pass is at the border with Thailand and that from there we could reach Bangkok. At the end, we arrived at the factory, where we met our friends who came in the first group; they asked why we had come, saying 'the jobs aren't here; we don't have good life here'. So, we told my friend, 'we came here because of your letter to your mother where you wrote that you have very good job and life here' and she said that she didn't want her mother and family to be worried about her so she didn't want to tell what the real situation was. Then we all got even more upset.

For those who venture beyond the border towns to reach the Bangkok area, the risk of being caught by police on the way to Bangkok is always there. May Aye, a Karen woman, came to Thailand with her mother, who used to be in a refugee camp, and who had been to Bangkok with the agent. Even though it was not her mother's first trip to Bangkok, they still faced the risk of being arrested by the police:

> I accompanied my mother to Mae Sot with the agent. The agent is from our village. He brought us to Mae Sot and after we had waited there for one week, we went on foot to Bangkok... The trip was very tough. We walked in the forest for five days. Then, when we arrived at Chiang Mai bus station, we got arrested... We were asked for money to be released. [But] we didn't have any money. One girl in our group had gold earrings but the police didn't accept those; instead they asked my mother to search for money.

The journey of migrant workers away from their familiar village often starts with a bumpy ride, both physically and psychologically – which prefigures the journey they will go through with work, with family, and with friends in the years to come.

Reconstructing families

Most Burmese women remain part of an extended family, and even after marriage they frequently live with their parents rather than their in-laws.[15] So leaving home to work in Thailand also means parting from family members, which can lead to significant changes in family relationships.

However, economic difficulties and the lack of opportunities in Burma are also changing the attitudes of the older generation, many of whom are encouraging their daughters and sons to go to Thailand to work, in spite of fears that migration will undermine the behaviour and values of their children. The women we spoke to who had left home against their parents' wishes acknowledged that the power of the older generation to make decisions about their children's future was becoming weaker. In most cases, however, the workers have to convince their parents before they are able to leave. Thet Htar Lwin, a Burman woman in her late twenties, came to Three Pagodas Pass on the recommendation of a neighbour. She faced strong opposition from her father, even though she was travelling with her husband.

> When I planned to come here [to Thailand], my father was very angry. He shouted at me saying, 'Go – go – do – do whatever you want, do it by yourself'. Even when the departure date was fixed and the car [to pick us up] had been reserved, he still refused to give me permission to leave... My father was crying. Now when my sister [who is] in Bangkok calls him, he says, 'Come home. I want all my daughters to come back to me. We are a family. If you don't have anything to eat, you can stay with me and we can eat together. You can live with me in times of scarcity as well as times of abundance.'

The parents' generation is strongly committed to the importance of education as the key to securing a better life within Burma, reflecting the investment in education and other benefits that were made during their own youth before the military government. However, the younger generation has no experience of education improving social mobility, as in previous eras, and is more convinced that working in Thailand rather than getting an education in Burma is the key to their future. May Thu Maw is a single Burman woman, who came to Thailand when she was in her mid-thirties. She worked for twelve years in a number of different garment factories near Yangon, but was then drawn by the higher wages available in Thailand, and wanted the rest of her family to join her. She explains how her aspirations conflicted with those of her parents' generation.

> I've tried to persuade my nieces to come and work here [in Three Pagodas Pass] as I was able to arrange for them to work in the footwear factory. But their mother as well as mine wanted them to stay in school and finish university, but I think they will need to find work even if they graduate; here I see many graduates who are

sewing in the garment factories. So why should my nieces waste their time in education? They should quit their education and start working early so they can support their family.

Given the isolation that Burmese people have suffered in recent decades as the military government has restricted travel and access to international media and the Internet, many older people are not familiar with the geography of the border towns to where their children migrate. Nandar Cho, who now works in Three Pagodas Pass, explains:

I told my husband and sisters but not my parents about my trip. I just told my parents I was going to the border to work in a sewing factory. In my town, people do not know much about the border – how far away the border is from the town and how to get there. And they don't know how tough the trip is... My parents don't know that I am here; they know that I left our town and went to join my friend but they don't know how far away I am – if they did they would worry about me and would have tried to stop me leaving. So I dare not phone them... I told [my husband] that I would go to Myawaddy because I didn't know where Three Pagodas Pass was, and in our town we have only heard about Myawaddy – that is the border town to work.

Even when they have given their permission, many parents are deeply ambivalent about their daughters leaving home to work in factories in Thailand. Mu Mu Han, a 20-year-old Burman woman, was happy working in a garment factory in Yangon, but her mother insisted that she went to Thailand to work so that she could save up to start her own business in Thailand. But once Mu Mu Han had left for Three Pagodas Pass her mother regretted her decision:

My mother asked me when I will visit her. She misses me and always cries on the phone. Although she [was the one who] told me to come [to Thailand to work], in reality she doesn't want me to be so far away from her. She regrets sending me here and told me to come back with others from my hometown. For me, although I miss them, I won't go back to visit – if I do my mother will not let me return [to Thailand] again.

Other parents manage to visit their working children in Thailand, often taking advantage of accessing opportunities to carry out petty trade based on selling smuggled goods in Burma. Mae Suu Aye, a Burman woman married to a Mon man whom she met in Mae Sot, said:

> [My husband] never goes back home. He is from Mawlamyaing. But his father comes here [to Mae Sot] and whenever he comes, my husband gives him some money and presents.

Phyu Phyu Cho came to Thailand four years ago, and now lives in Mae Sot with her husband and three children. Two of her three siblings are in Thailand and her mother goes back and forth between them:

> My mother is coming and going back all the time – she is now an expert in coming and going. Even when I was in Yangon, mother came there once a month to buy clothes in the big market and sold them back in her village, or brought them to Mae Sot to sell. She also buys clothes from Mae Sot to sell in Yangon or in her village.

Going to work in Thailand is a significant deviation from the 'protection' Burmese young women traditionally received from their parents and family. The possibility of working in Thailand has shaken the ways in which both generations are constructing their identities and the narratives of their desired futures. The ambivalence seen in the testimonies of both migrant women workers and their parents show that the whole family – those who are moving and those left behind – go through a process of rethinking their values and outlook. The changing relationship between the young migrant workers and their parents/families back home is also reflected in their remittance behaviour.

Remittances as obligation

One of the ways in which migrants maintain their connections with their families is through remitting money from their wages earned in Thailand. There is a general expectation that all migrants will support their families, but our research indicates that the pattern of remittances varies, and reflects the changing relationship between the migrants and their families back home. But for women migrants, in particular, their remittance behaviour is determined not only by the financial needs of their families but also by their changing sense of obligation to their families

Most migrants from Burma do not have access to regular financial services, because they are not legally registered in Thailand, or have not registered their departure with the authorities at home, or come from remote areas where financial service coverage is non-existent. The majority tend to use a range of informal channels to send money back to their families. The most common is what is termed *Hundi*,[16] which is a network of dealers or brokers who transfer money between different places. The Burmese migrants generally refer to them as 'agents'[17] and hand over Thai currency, which is transferred to partners in Burma, who then deliver the money in Burmese kyat to the families. The advantage for the workers is that agents do not charge a fee for this service, although they do manipulate the baht/kyat exchange rate to their advantage, often engage in cross-border trade. Agents in Mae Sot can be readily found in the market and collect cash directly from the workers; however, the workers in Bangkok are required to transfer the money to the agent's bank account in border towns, forcing those without bank accounts themselves to utilise those of friends. These services are costly, and so workers tend to save up to send a lump sum, and family members often combine their savings in order to minimise the cost of remitting.

The other informal mode of remittance is to give the cash to a 'carrier' (who migrant workers call a *'carry'*), who physically transports the money, along with other gifts, to the families back in Burma. Although this is an apparently less secure mode of transfer, migrants have considerable confidence in this system since the carriers involved are known to the home communities, which are often too remote to be served by agents. Also many migrant workers send money back through friends and relatives, especially women migrants, who also use the opportunity to send consumer items such as clothes and cooking oil along with the money, though this is more difficult for those working in the centre of Thailand. Some migrants use bank transfers within Burma, especially those in Mae Sot, who can cross to Myawaddy and use the Burmese banks, which charge less than Thai banks or agents; however, the workers who use these banks do incur costs crossing the border. Our research indicates that women are more willing than men to spend the time and money required to use bank transfers.

Women's remittance behaviour differs from men's in other ways as well. Migrants on average manage to send up to 15,000 Thai baht per year. Although women earn 20 per cent less than men, we found that they are more consistent remitters than men, though they tend to send smaller amounts. Also, like any other migrant community, the longer migrants are out of their own country, the more likely are they to stop sending money to their families, but women migrant workers in Thailand tend to maintain their remittances much longer than their male counterparts.[18]

For women migrants the web of obligations, duty and support underlying their patterns of remittance are complex, and are closely linked to their own changing circumstances and priorities. As single women, most migrants see their primary obligation to be to their parents. Thin Thin Myint, a Burman woman from Pegu in her early twenties, came to Mae Sot with her older sister. She used to work in Yangon, and her parents had moved there in order to be close to the daughters. After she came to Mae Sot, she maintained close contact with her parents and sends money to them:

> We never expect our parents to save for us because our intention in working here is to pay back our debt to our parents who nurtured us very well until we grew up.

Some young women see their earnings in Thailand as part of an ongoing family accumulation strategy, which they still feel very much part of. Tin Moe Aung is the youngest of five siblings, and is the only one who came to Thailand to work:

My parents are old and I would like them to spend [the remittances] for their health, food and for donations [to the temple]. They are farmers and they also buy more land as investment. We have our own house so we don't need to build a house, and I don't want to go back at the moment... My parents have said I can stop sending them money and save for myself if I like, because they are already better off after receiving my remittances, but I would like to keep sending money to them so that they can use it as they wish.

There is often mutuality in the remittance relationship; family members call on migrant workers when they are in need of money, but equally migrant workers receive financial support during difficult times, when they are short of money if things are not going so well, or to cover the costs of visits home. Pwint Phyu Maw reported that she and her sisters, all working in garment factories in Mae Sot, were relying on support from their mother. She used to earn well and was initially able to remit. However, when orders started to dwindle due to a labour dispute in the factory, she lost her job and instead started to sew at home, but her income was not enough for her to support herself. When she and her sisters had been able to send substantial sums home, her mother would play the lottery. Now her daughters are struggling and so she has stopped gambling and now has to support her daughters in Mae Sot:

At the moment, I'm asking for money from my mother. My mother came to see me last week and gave us money. She also brought some rice for my two sisters. She will send more rice with my youngest sister, who is coming to Mae Sot next week. Now we are in a situation where we have to ask for money back from the parents instead of remitting money to them.

Marriage, children and changing relationships

It is not only changes in the employment and earning situation of workers that necessitate support from home. Women workers, in particular those who become wives and mothers while they are in Thailand, need to find ways to manage their multiple roles, and frequently need their families' support, particularly to care for young infants and school-age children. If there are several siblings working in Thailand, it is generally the oldest (most often the oldest daughter) who collects the remittances from other family members and takes responsibility for sending the money back home. Siblings tend to exert pressure on each other to maintain remittances; however, this pressure diminishes after marriage when many migrants reduce the amount they send home, or even stop altogether. However, the situation frequently changes when they have children, as May Nwe Nwe Kyaw explains:

After finishing paying off my debt, which took a year, I called [my siblings] to come here. They didn't have to borrow money for the travel cost like me because I advanced them money [16,000 baht each]. They came here five months ago and luckily they got jobs immediately. Now they are paying me their debt back little by little because they have to send money to our parents. I can't send money to my parents as I have my own family now. Let my single siblings work here and send money home to our parents. My husband and I have to send 500,000 kyat per year through an agent to my parents-in-law, who take care of my children for schooling, food, clothing and so on.

Mae Suu Aye has six siblings, though only one brother is in Mae Sot with her. Whilst living in there she got married and had a child, but she regrets not being able to remit any more.

After having a child I can't afford to remit. Before I had my child, I remitted as much as I could; I remitted like 50,000 kyat or 100,000 kyat at a time. Sometimes I sent seasoning powders, detergents – whatever my family needed. Now it is only work and eat... [My parents] don't say anything [when I don't remit]... They never ask me to remit unless they really need money urgently. (Mae Su Aye of Mae Sot)

Burmese families have different expectations of remittances from sons and daughters. It is socially acceptable that men do not remit after getting married. Yin Min told us she was very upset and disappointed when her older brother, who had been supporting the family through his remittances, got married. Because she knew that now his priority would be his new family – his wife and future children – she quit school herself and came to Thailand to work. However, some 90 per cent of the women in our survey continue to send money to their families after marriage, compared to only 60 per cent of the men.

Sometimes young women continue to remit money to their parents after marriage because they are aware that their parents would not approve of their marriage, often entered into very quickly because they find the changes in their lives after migration, including loneliness and absence of family authority, too difficult to cope with. Mi Mi Hlaing Chaw was faced with a dilemma; she kept the news of her marriage from her mother, so she had no acceptable reason for discontinuing her remittances, yet she could not afford to maintain the payments. But even women whose marriage is acknowledged by their families strive to maintain remittances to their parental households, often because they need their mothers or sisters to take care of their children. They will also send money to the husband's family and to other family members, either because their own family cannot provide childcare or because they want to maintain economic ties with the extended family back home. As Hnin Zarchi Htwe, who has worked in Samut Prakan for a number of years, explains:

> I arranged an ATM card with the help of my employer. My husband and I both put money in the account and remit money to Burma as we have two children living with my parents. The children are attending the school in Taung-gyi. We remitted 500,000 kyat in the last 2-3 months. We send money in turn to both sides of the family. I also send money to my younger sister, who has a business in Burma renting phones to businessmen... I receive some profit from this business. But it is not a regular income.

Notably our data indicate that over half of our respondents stopped sending money home after they had their first child. But of those had continued to remit, 65 per cent had sent their pre-school or school-aged children back to their families in Burma, so they needed to cover the cost of looking after them. If economic circumstances force them to stop sending money home, many women are deeply ashamed of their inability to fulfil their obligations to their families. Thet Htar Lwin needed to pay a lot for her initial settlement in Three Pagodas Pass. Although her parents do not ask her to remit, and even tell her to come back to Burma if she is not happy in Thailand, she is determined to make it in Thailand:

> I feel bad. You know – I've heard that my sister remits all the time. But I can't, and I feel very inferior... But I don't have the money so how can I remit? Oh, I want to remit so much that I feel like dying and when I feel bad I don't work for 3-4 days.

Such feelings are exacerbated when the family is already caring for the children, and women frequently resort to borrowing from moneylenders in order to maintain their financial obligations. In the case of Phyu Pyu Cho, a garment worker in Three Pagodas Pass, this has affected her health. The pressures come not just from family obligations but also from gossiping neighbours:

> Sometimes I remitted by borrowing money here with interest. But it is not always easy to borrow money; if [I] could not borrow money then I just explain to my mother and she understands. My children are there [with her] to be fed, and she had to find [money] and I felt bad. My mother looked after my children and I could not send her any money. This gave me a headache before the end of every month as I was worried because I needed to send money to my mother. Thinking of how my mother would look after my children without [my] remittances to her! How would she feed them? That was always in my mind. Of course they [the neighbours] gossiped and said bad things to us as well as boasting about their children to my mother. Some people said bad things to me, accusing me of 'keeping the children with your mother and starving your mother'.

It is clear that the relations between migrant workers and their families are complex and change over time. Filial obligation would seem to be broken by marriage and children, as women prioritise their own families and futures. But since women so often need to lean on their families for childcare, and since it is so difficult to keep their children with them while they are working long shifts in the factory, their sending of money home is transformed from daughterly piety to financial necessity to meet children's expenses.

Women's journeys: agency, subordination and change

The voices of the migrant women workers cited above show how diverse are their reasons for leaving home and travelling far away from their original villages. Their journeys necessitate them being distant from their families as well as from their homes and communities. But their motivations for leaving home are complex, shaped by both the structural situation and their personal aspirations and experiences. As Lee explains, in her study of women workers in South China, the workers' construction and understanding of their own identities are shaped by 'people's temporally and spatially variable place in culturally constructed stories composed of (breakable) rules, (variable) practices binding (and unbinding) institutions and the multiple plots of family, nation or economic life'.[19] The journeys of the young Burmese women which are the focus of this book reflect the changes in these culturally constructed stories about their role and responsibilities in the family, their individual desires to break free of family control and seek alternative futures, and their acquisition of different responsibilities as wives and mothers.

However, as we explore in the following chapters, it is an irony that, once they have established independent lives of their own by migrating for work, getting married and having their own children, they frequently have to rely on their families at their place of origin, since there are insurmountable difficulties in combining their factory work with the demands of caring for their children. For Burmese women factory workers, the standard story of migration as a source of support for impoverished families at home is complicated by considerations of gender and reproduction; financial remittances are frequently exchanged for care services, forcing closer ongoing links with home, at the very point at which women are seeking to establish more autonomy for themselves and their families.

4

Migrant women in Thailand's factories: working conditions, struggles and experiences

The conditions in which Burmese migrant workers live and work are exploitative and difficult by any standard. But the women we spoke to in the border factories and in the interior of the countries are willing to put up with what they know are illegal working conditions and labour regimes in order to continue to earn money for themselves and their families. To do this they have to adapt to an underground world of contacts, agents, factory owners and managers, as well as the police, immigration and military personnel on either side of the border. As we have seen, the workers come from all over Burma. The majority of those to whom we spoke came from the border states and the central regions, which are towards the south-eastern part of Burma and have relatively good transportation links to Thailand. However, some had travelled from as far away as Rakhine and Chin states, which are on the Western border with Bangladesh. Migrant factory workers are in general relatively well educated and literate and able to understand the iniquities of their working and living situation. Whilst there is a preponderance of young single women among the garment factory workers, there are also many women who are already married when they first migrate to Thailand. In some cases, as we have shown in Chapter 3, migration is a household strategy, and families have sold property or incurred debt in order to finance the migratory journey. In other cases migrants have friends and relatives already working in Thailand; in others, (usually) young women come against their parents' wishes. The diversity of their backgrounds is matched also by a wide variation in the experiences they have, their perceptions of these experiences, how they are able to cope with difficulties, and the pressure from family back home. In this chapter, we describe the work-related experience of these migrant workers.

Who are the women workers?

According to official statistics there are slightly more Burmese migrant men than women in Thailand. However, women greatly outnumber men in the factories, and most accounts report that women comprise up to 80 per cent of the workforce, though there is some variation since men are more likely to be hired in the knitwear factories, which have more complex and modern machinery. The ages of the factory workers range from 15 to 70 years old, although we did meet even younger Burmese women, particularly in Three Pagodas Pass, who were having difficulty finding jobs because they were too small to be able to sit and operate the sewing machines.

Because of the insecurity and precariousness of the occupations in which they work, most migrant workers change jobs frequently, often moving as much as five times in two or three years, in spite of the fact that registration of temporary migrant workers is linked to specific employers, and workers risk losing their official status once they change job. Women tend to move to other garment factories, or to leather or fish processing plants, and sometimes to other occupations, such as domestic work, cleaning, agricultural labour and working in shops and restaurants. If migrant workers have acquired skills in garment factories either in Burma or in Thailand, they generally try to stick to sewing or machine knitting jobs, but when this is not possible they switch to other types of employment. So classification of workers, as either domestic workers or factory workers, or farm workers, is not very accurate since migrants tend to move between these occupations.

Our research indicates that some 90 per cent of both female and male workers in the locations near Bangkok had registration documents; in contrast, less than 5 per cent of those surveyed in Three Pagodas Pass had official documentation, reflecting the ease with which they were able to cross daily over the border. In Mae Sot, at the time of our research, less than 50 per cent of the workers we surveyed were registered. The different levels of registration reflect the variations in official surveillance in each of the three locations. In Three Pagodas Pass there were few reports of police raids or deportation of unregistered workers, and even those who did stay on the Thai side felt secure, whereas in Mae Sot, although the checking of migrant workers is not as strict as in Bangkok, there are many formal and informal checkpoints. According to local sources, when the registration system was first introduced more men than women migrants registered. This was partly because families could not afford to pay the fees for all workers, and tended to give priority to men on the assumption that their jobs and lives require them to have more visibility and mobility within public spaces, and therefore be more vulnerable to arrest and detention. After the nationality verification and temporary passport process was introduced in 2010 almost 90 per cent of all workers we talked to in Bangkok had applied for their passports, financed mostly by employers advancing the costs and then deducting them from the workers' wages. However, only 40 per cent of those in Mae Sot and none of the Three Pagodas Pass workers had applied. The introduction of temporary passports has appeared to reduce the incentive for workers in the borderlands to obtain legal status. According to the workers, Mae Sot employers are unwilling to assist since the procedure is more complicated and expensive compared to the former registration system, and according to the employers workers can hide on the other side of the river in the event of a police raid. Khin Mar Hlaing, a Muslim

from Karen state, who works as an interpreter as well as in a
factory office, told us:

> Nowadays, none of the riverside factories' makes ID card for their
> workers. You know, what my boss said, *I neh nee nee lay, lar pan
> yin pyay paw* ('it is so close to the river bank [border], so when the
> police come to arrest them, the workers can just run'). Most of the
> bosses from the riverside factories have this kind of perception.
> Right now you look at who is applying for temporary passport – it's
> only the Bangkok workers. We here [in Mae Sot] are not interested.
> The boss said that we are very close [to Burma], so if something
> happens, we can just run.

The fees charged by agents to organise temporary passports
and work permits are high, since the procedures and required
documents are much more complicated than the requirements of
the earlier registration system. Workers are also reluctant to enter
into this process, not just because of the cost but also because they
are required to obtain household registration documents from
their original village. They fear that once the Burmese authorities
know which households have members working in Thailand, they
will punish their families by levying additional taxation or other
measures. Some of them said that they preferred to leave their jobs
rather than go through the process of nationality verification, and
risk problems for their relatives at home.

It was not uncommon for the factory managers to create a
parallel system for their workers. San San Swe, together with her
four sisters, has been working in Mae Sot for six years.

> If we are checked [by the police] at the checkpoint, we don't need to
> pay. The factory owner can deal with the police. But we have to keep
> this pink card with us so that the police will know that we are from
> this factory. Sometimes, we just need to show [the police] our factory
> card which we use for receiving our wages. If we forget to bring our
> factory card we stay at the police checkpoint and call our friends
> to bring our cards. When we show the police our factory card they
> let us go, but this only applies to the police checkpoint nearby our
> factory and not for all the checkpoints and police in Mae Sot.

There are various reasons why many workers remain unregistered even after the new system based on the bilateral MOU was introduced. Some fail to make the application within the designated registration period; others complain that they have been denied assistance or cooperation by their employers. Many do not have enough money to pay the not inconsiderable charges required. If they have moved to a new employer (thus invalidating any work permit they may have previously obtained) or have been ill or pregnant during the registration period, they are effectively unavailable for employment, and thus ineligible to register. As of March 2011, 762,640 workers had either registered or initiated the nationality verification process.[2] This means that less than half of the estimated 2-3 million migrant workers in Thailand have been involved in some kind of a process to document their status.

What kind of factories do they work in?

The factories that employ migrant workers in the three areas we investigated were mainly garment factories – both those sewing up cotton pieces into final garments and those fabricating knitted articles from yarn. But there was some variation; in Three Pagodas Pass there were also subcontractors making trainers and other sportswear for global brands, as well as the factories manufacturing mosquito nets.

As we noted in Chapter 2 there was a high concentration of factories employing migrant workers in Tak province, where Mae Sot is located, accounting for over 13 per cent of the total number of registered Burmese workers in Thailand in 2006,[3] though the actual numbers including non-registered migrant workers were likely to have been double that number. The garment factories in Mae Sot are generally subcontracted to enterprises which carry out most of the production process in other parts of Thailand. All the knitting factories produce for export, while the CMT (cut, make and trim) garment output is divided between the domestic market and international markets, which include North America, Japan,

Europe and China. According to the local Employment Office, there were approximately 22,000 workers employed in Mae Sot's factories in 2007, and twenty of the formally registered larger companies also operated factories in Bangkok. A spokesperson from the FTUB calculated that some 60 per cent of the factories are owned by foreign companies (including entrepreneurs from Hong Kong and Taiwan). One of the garment companies has two smaller plants elsewhere in Thailand, but the Mae Sot factory employs five times as many workers as either of its other two establishments. In the Mae Sot factory all the production workers are Burmese, whereas the other factories employed some Thai workers. The Tak Provincial Labour Office estimated that there were 100 large establishments employing Burmese migrant workers, with a further 100, including home-based factories, which employed fewer than thirty workers. However, there is a high turnover of factories, with constant changes in ownership and business failures and start-ups in response to fluctuations in orders, so it is difficult to determine the precise number.

One of the largest garment factories in Mae Sot employs 2,500 workers (2,100 Burmese and 400 Thai), of which 90 per cent are women. Some 30 per cent of the production is for export and the rest is for the higher middle domestic market. Raw materials are brought in from Bangkok and finished goods are transported back to the capital every day, with a fleet of ten large and six medium-sized trucks. The owner of the factory was confident that the garments produced in Mae Sot were competitive with products from China. He claimed that although wages have historically been lower in China, the actual labour cost in Mae Sot is lower than the comparable costs in the Chinese province of Yunnan. He insisted that Mae Sot can produce higher quality products and has a better record of meeting delivery targets, though he complained about not being able to retain trained migrant workers: 'this place is like a training ground to prepare Burmese migrant workers to go and get jobs in central cities.' He considered that the situation has got worse after the introduction of temporary passports under the

MOU, as factories in Bangkok are hiring more workers previously employed in Mae Sot, which has facilitated the mobility of migrant workers away from the border, resulting in difficulties for the larger factories in Mae Sot recruiting registered workers.

The Bangkok factories only started to employ Burmese workers in significant numbers around 2002, when the booming economy meant that demand for factory workers outstripped supply. According to one estimate, there were 20,120 registered migrant workers in Samut Prakan province in 2007.[4] We visited a fairly large textile and garment factory there which had employed its first Burmese migrant workers only in late 2005. In this factory only 10 per cent of its 900-strong workforce were Burmese, who were all employed as casual day labourers. The rationale for the company's hiring policy gives us an insight into the differentiation of the labour market between Thai and migrant workers. This is a formal export factory that meets a range of international standards such as SA 8000 (labour), ISO 9000 (quality) and ISO 14000 (environment). Some 40 per cent of this factory's product is for export, and their product is for high-end markets. The rationale for employing Burmese migrant workers, according to the human resources manager, is that 'Thai people don't want to work in the textile factory, especially making thread. There are bad working conditions with long days; they have to stand the whole day, and it is noisy, dusty and dangerous.' This factory operates twenty-four hours a day, and has three shifts, which is unpopular among workers since it allows no opportunity for overtime work. In the face of these conditions, the turnover among Thai workers is high, whereas the Burmese workers tend to stay longer and, according to this manager, are more hard-working. However, there are sections where Burmese workers are unable to work because their lack of Thai language skills means that they cannot follow orders and patterns. Unlike in Mae Sot, where many managers can speak Burmese (or are Burmese themselves), the use of the Thai language is crucial in and around Bangkok. However, the human resources manager told us that it was proving

difficult to expand the recruitment of registered Burmese workers, causing some factories to close down, and others to extend
recruitment to workers currently in Mae Sot. The manager found
Burmese workers docile and easy to manage: 'Burmese workers
help sustain the factory. They are hard-working, follow orders,
and do not complain. Since their situation here is better than in
Burma the migrant workers do not envy Thais, and thus do not
go on strike.'

There were no factories employing migrant workers in Three
Pagodas Pass before 2005, but their numbers have grown rapidly
since, and in 2007 there were approximately eighty manufacturing
establishments in and around this border town, with estimates of
the number of workers employed ranging from 3,300 to 13,000.[5]
There are only three or four larger factories, which employ up to
1,000 workers, with perhaps another ten employing up to 100
workers, whilst the remainder are small enterprises with only
twenty to fifty workers, though some workers suggested that many
owners prefer to operate in a number of small factories rather than
running a large consolidated enterprise. Recently a dozen or so
small factories have been established on the Burmese side of the
border, and this would appear to be a growing trend because of
increasing pressure on space in the Thai town of Three Pagodas
Pass, which has pushed up rents. Also on the Thai side, there have
been some factories built recently outside the town, requiring the
provision of a van service to transport commuting workers from
the town to the factory location.

Working conditions

In July 2007, we held a workshop with migrant workers and
members of NGOs and trade unions in Mae Sot, where we discussed
at length the problems they identified and their complaints about
their working conditions. The outcome of these discussions, and of
further consultations during 2008 and 2009 with workers in the
other research sites, revealed a set of issues which corresponded

to studies done by other researchers in this area – namely, low wages, excessively long working hours, no holiday time, threats by employers to report unregistered workers to the police and have them deported, confiscation of identity documents, lack of awareness of workers' rights, discrimination in terms of wage payments and allocation of easier or more lucrative tasks on the production line (particularly related to piece-rate systems), no freedom of communication (referring to restricted use of mobile phones), restricted physical mobility, no job and social security, no life insurance, minimal access to health-care services, absence of trade-union representation and poor living conditions.[6]

The working hours are very long in the border factories, which leaves the women hardly any time for themselves. A typical working day is 8 a.m. to 5 p.m., and then 6 to 9 p.m., with two thirty-minute breaks, although if there are pressing deadlines shifts can extend until midnight or later. However, the workers do not necessarily seek shorter working hours, since this often implies that orders are limited and workers do not have the opportunity to do overtime. Workers generally only get two days off per month,[7] but since the non-working days generally fall just after their fortnightly payday, a good proportion of their 'free' time is spent shopping and arranging to send money and goods to their families back home.

Although some factories supply food with the dormitory accommodation, most of the women workers to whom we spoke preferred to organise their own shopping and cooking. During their breaks, they were able to buy vegetables from informal sellers in front of the factory, and then cook food using the rudimentary facilities in their dorms; they also had to fit in other tasks including cleaning, laundry, and bathing within their break periods. Married women in particular complained that their working day was too long, since in addition to their work in the factories they had to do a considerable amount of domestic work. Workers who are also wives and mothers complained that they were unable to take sufficient rest, let alone have any free time for leisure activities.[8]

Long working days clearly take their toll on women workers. San San Swe, with her six years experience of working in factories in Mae Sot, told us that

> I do not sew, but I work in quality control. I have to work standing the whole day... They don't let QC and workers who cut threads sit – only sewing workers can sit. They said if we sit we do not work properly... I earn 70 baht a day. For overtime I earn 8½ baht an hour. We have overtime until 12 p.m. and sometimes until 2 or 3 a.m... We can't sleep well. If we finish at 2 a.m., we only get to bed at 3 a.m. because we have to wash and eat first, and then we have to get up at 6 a.m. again to work the next morning... Sometimes if I feel sick, I have to take a day's leave but they don't like us to do that. In the sewing section the workers are very hard-working; they don't take breaks and during lunch time, they just eat and come back to work. Often in the afternoon or at night time, the supervisor has to shut down the electricity to make them stop sewing. In the morning, they start sewing at 6:30 a.m., even before the manager arrives – they want to sew more to earn more.

But the work is not stable and some of the jobs are very heavy, so many workers strive to please the supervisors in order to be allocated lighter tasks:

> Sometimes there are few orders, especially in the sewing sections. My sister's section did not have any work last month. She got only 2,000 baht that month... In our factory the workers who give the manager and the supervisor presents will get the easier sewing jobs. If we don't give them gifts the supervisor will give us difficult jobs, which take a long time to finish, so we can't earn as much. (San San Swe in Mae Sot)

Such heavy workloads take a toll on the workers' health, and many women complain of aching limbs and backs. But they fear they will lose their registration status – or even their job – if they take sick leave to recover. The experience of Marlar Kyaw, who went to Yangon to work in a garment factory after her mother died when she was 12 and now works at the big footwear factory in Three Pagodas Pass, is typical:

In the footwear factory, one girl got ill and she took one day's leave. The next day she went to work but she still felt ill so she took leave for another day. Then the manager told her to rest until she got better but that she would have to start again as a new worker when she recovered… She was crying – she had worked there for three years, and was earning 90 baht a day. If she started as a new worker her pay would go down to 60 baht a day. The factory didn't take into consideration her [past] contributions. So she will not work there any more.

It is not only that the work is hard and long; it also can be quite insecure. May Thin Aye was born in Karen state. When the fighting between the State Peace and Development Council (SPDC) and the Karen National Union (KNU) intensified, the whole family moved to Yangon, where she continued to study. But she then left school and went to work in a garment factory because of her family's financial situation. Then she came to Mae Sot with her sisters. Her story illustrates the range of problems that workers face:

We only earned 700 baht a month in the factory, which was not enough to survive in Mae Sot. Then with the help of friends and neighbours, we got a new job in another factory… Payments at that factory were regular. We [my sisters and I] earned 1,700 baht a month each and could remit 100,000 kyats a month to our parents regularly… After working there for two years, there was a police raid in our factory and we had to flee and the factory was closed down. So we had to get another job in a factory – this time in Mae Pa (on the outskirts of Mae Sot). In this factory, the owner did not provide accommodation so we had to rent a room outside. One day when we were returning from work at 2 a.m. after working overtime, the road was deserted – we witnessed a girl from our factory being robbed. We were too scared to go to work the next day. We remembered the face of that man who robbed the girl. Later we met him in the noodle shop and it was clear that he had not been punished. The last garment factory we worked in did not pay us properly. At first we had regular payments, but later the employer lied to us. We could not speak or understand much Thai. There was a change in the factory ownership and our employer told us that he gave the money for our wages to the new factory owner, but he denied getting it so we did not get any wages for the time we had worked and weren't able to send anything to our parents.

Some women were able to improve their earnings even though the situation was unstable. Thin Moe Aung has changed jobs at least four times since she came to Three Pagodas Pass six years ago. At first, the pay received in each factory was high, since they only hired when they had large orders. However, as soon as orders dropped off her earnings started to decrease. Her experience taught her that

> When the work was scarce it is worthwhile working for a daily rate, but not when orders are plentiful, especially for skilled workers. Since I am a skilled machinist, I can sew whatever clothes that come in, so I can earn more on piece rate than I would if I worked on a daily rate. Moreover, I feel much freer than when I was paid at a daily rate because then the owner controlled us all the time and we could not take a break when we wanted to.

Other women workers, especially those who had small children, preferred to take the work to their houses and work as home-based workers. Khin Myint Aung in Mae Sot told us that she earns 25 baht for finishing 100 garments for a nearby factory. She is able to manage about 170 items per day, giving her a daily rate of 42.5 baht, but this work is very irregular and often requires the assistance of other family members to reach this level of earning.

Although there were repeated complaints about the restricted meal breaks, long working hours, and limited days off, many migrant workers reported that working conditions were even worse in factories in Burma, where supervision is much stricter, working hours even longer, and wages even lower. In Thailand their main grievance concerned delayed or withheld wages, rather than working conditions. This is actually a reflection of the level of their exploitation; if they cannot be certain that they will be paid for the work they have done, they see little point in airing extensive complaints about working conditions. They are also well aware that they have little prospect of changing their situation. Under Thai law foreign workers can join Thai trade unions, but may not hold office or organise their own unions or other organisations.[9] Although there are a number of NGOs in Thailand that work to support migrant workers in claiming their (limited) legal rights and that have been successful in landmark cases which have also brought the plight of the migrant workers to public attention,[10] the majority of migrant workers within Thailand continue to exist beyond the protection of the law.

Security of employment and mobility

Migrant workers in Thailand face a series of obstacles if they wish to change their job. Although legal registration in theory allows them to register with a new employer, in practice the system is stacked against them. Factory managers and owners routinely retain possession of all the migrants' original documents, including temporary registration and work permits, which gives them unlimited power. For their part the workers are afraid that if they leave, their current employer will inform the police, and they will risk arrest and deportation because they would then not be in possession of legal documents. Punpuing and Jampaklay et al.[11] reported that 40 per cent of the migrant factory workers they interviewed said that their original documents were confiscated, and nearly 80 per cent feared being arrested by the police. It is not uncommon for migrant workers, particularly women, to stay inside the factory compound in order to avoid harassment from the authorities. The same survey showed that 64 per cent of employers believed that migrants should be locked up at night to prevent them from escaping.

Migrant workers' fears of arrest are well founded; they face not only deportation but also routine abuse when they are arrested. A report from the Mekong Migration Network and Asian Migration Centre[12] detailed widespread abuse of detained migrant workers, including intrusive full-body searches and the physical molestation of women migrants, such as cutting short their traditionally worn long hair, on the pretext that this will deter them from re-entering the country after deportation. Official registration does not protect migrant workers from detention, especially when they do not have their original documents in their possession. But even when they do carry the appropriate documentation, they are still not safe from arrest. A worker we interviewed in Bangkok recalled how a Thai policeman threatened to tear up his legal documentation, indicating that the reality for migrant workers is little protection from arbitrary and degrading treatment by police and other authorities.

Under the current MOU system, registration cards and temporary passports are both tied to proof of employment, so that a migrant worker wishing to change job needs a letter from the current employer indicating his willingness to release him or her. In practice this has proved to be near impossible to obtain, especially when the worker wishes to leave because of problems at the workplace. So there is usually no option other than to leave without agreement, which means that the worker will lose his or her current registration card. There have been some cases in Mae Sot where a new employer has been sympathetic and supported the re-registration of the worker, though this is not a common experience, and is unknown in the factories around Bangkok.

The registration documents themselves also include restrictions on workers' mobility, officially requiring them to remain within the boundaries of the district in which they are registered. But restrictions on moving job exacerbate the insecurity caused by the precariousness of workers' employment. Registration documents in themselves are no guarantee of the continuation of employment with a particular employer, nor do they ensure the payment of the minimum wage, or limitation of working hours, or any other benefits. Although registered workers are entitled to complain to the Labour Protection Office, they have little real protection from the law and face almost insurmountable difficulties if they wish to improve their situation.

Accommodation and food

The housing available to migrant workers in Thailand reflects their temporary and irregular status, as well as the particular nature of the local labour market. In Mae Sot most single women and men live in factory accommodation within the factory compound, which is frequently the cheapest and most convenient, though families are required to rent accommodation in the town. The accommodation we visited in May 2008 in some of the larger factories in Mae Sot resembled third-class train sleeper cabins, with two- or three-storeyed bunk beds, divided from the next room by a thin wooden partition or curtain. Workers are required to keep all their personal possessions in a space little bigger than 8 square foot, where they also carry out all their food preparation and domestic activities; no mosquito nets are provided, even though this area is still considered a malaria risk. The dormitories can be sited inside or outside of the compound. In the particular accommodation we visited, the bathroom and toilet area was inside the factory compound, and the sleeping accommodation was outside, which is a further inconvenience for workers who have a limited time to fulfil all their personal needs. This factory provided some basic foodstuff in return for compulsory wage deductions, but the workers complained that this consisted of the same curry served twice a day, resulting in many workers choosing to cook their own food at additional expense.

Thin Thin Myint shared with three other workers a 10 square foot room in a two-storey concrete building in Mae Sot, which was divided into a number of rooms by wooden partitions. The workers had to pay rent to the factory manager, who had himself rented the building from a Thai businessman, as well as a compulsory 150 baht levy to the local police to allow them to stay there. Tin Nwe Soe reported that she and two other women shared a cramped concrete-floored space in Mae Sot, which was too small to sleep stretched out. The room was only separated from others by thick papers and cloth; it was only 5 foot high, so she also has to keep her head bowed when she was in her room. Accommodation for men and women was not separate in this building, and the upper part of Tin Nwe Soe's room was occupied by male workers, with only a thin layer of wood to separate the different sleeping spaces. Such cramped accommodation, remote from washing and toilet

facilities, creates major problems for the women workers. San San
Swe in Mae Sot noted:

> Oh [the accommodation is] very dirty. In the afternoon we have
> to rush to take a bath. Sometimes the water we have collected [for
> ourselves to use] is used by others. We have to collect water for our
> own use otherwise there is no water left in our breaks. When the
> workers are cooking there is not enough electricity for the factory,
> so we are now only allowed to use charcoal, or can club together to
> buy a gas stove.

Workers who are married or wish to live with other family
members or friends in independent accommodation have to fend
for themselves, and many live in quite primitive circumstances.
Sandar Aye has to work at home sewing garments whilst looking
after her 2-year-old son. Her husband still had a job at a garment
factory but his wages had become irregular because the factory
owner routinely delayed paying or underpaid him, so they had to
move into even more inferior accommodation:

> Our place is owned by a Thai who let Burmese people build huts on
> his land. We don't pay rent but we don't have water and electricity
> there. We use candles at night and we have to buy water from the
> owner of the nearby tube well. Everyone here is a relative or friend of
> my sister, and we have managed to establish our own community.

Shopping and cooking food are major challenges for migrant
workers, given their low and irregular wages; those in Mae Sot
often have to rely on credit from Burmese traders, for which they
are generally charged 20 per cent interest per month. In Three
Pagodas Pass the situation is different as most migrant workers
commute daily to Thailand from the Burmese side of the border.
However, their situation is not without problems. The workers are
in the main migrants from other areas within Burma and therefore
have to pay specific charges levied by the local Burmese authorities,
including 20 baht a month each for fire security fees and guest fees
(payable in Thai baht because that is is the currency in circulation
on the Burmese side of the Three Pagodas Pass border), as well

as compulsory contributions for specific projects such as building pagodas, maintaining schools and repairing monasteries. In addition, they have to pay for daily transport to the border, which costs 20 baht return. Since there is little available accommodation on the Thai side of the border, workers have little choice. If they have to work late to meet urgent production orders, they stay overnight inside the factories sleeping on the floor. There are reports that some small home-based factories offer better accommodation, with couples able to occupy one room in the upstairs of the factory. As in Mae Sot, workers frequently seek collective – if primitive – solutions to the challenges of their situation. Mu Mu Han has organised a system of collective shopping and cooking with friends:

> We collect 10 baht a day from each person and cook curries and rice in a rice cooker, which we eat together. We go to the market once a week – the Friday one. We don't need to pay for accommodation, electricity and water. We cook with wood fuel which the men cut for us and sometimes they cook for us as well.

In Bangkok the factories do not provide accommodation, so workers are forced to rent rooms in the local area, leading to clusters of slum settlements. Because their accommodation is generally some distance from the factories they are not able to cook for themselves during their working day, and have to rely on the often inferior and expensive food provided by the employers, or purchase food from street vendors.

Pay and deductions

The low level of wages, as well as delayed or non-payment of wages, was a frequent and central complaint from the workers, particularly those in Mae Sot. The minimum wage rate in Mae Sot is some 70 per cent of the rate prevailing in Bangkok. But migrant workers rarely receive the full minimum wage rate. Migrant workers in Tak province earned only 50–80 baht per day in 2006,[13] which was between 38 and 69 per cent of the prevailing minimum wage rate of 130 baht, and only half the daily wage rate for migrant workers in Bangkok. The reasons for these very low wages are complex; partly they are due to the prevalence of low-paid and seasonal work for migrants in the agricultural sector; but they also appear to reflect the relative freedom of border factories to flout minimum wage levels. Subsequent research reported that in 2008 only one of the 400-plus factories in Mae Sot was paying the provincial minimum wage, and the average daily wage was only 70 baht.[14] According to labour inspection officers it is often difficult to detect the underpayment of wages, because whereas on the books workers are paid the minimum wage, the actual payment they receive is far lower, as we explore below. This is compounded by the fact that many workers in Mae Sot are on piece rates, so that when orders are low this is directly reflected in their level of earnings. Workers reported that a few factory owners provide workers with a sum of 20 baht a day for food if there is no work, but there is no contractual obligation to pay anything if the factory is idle.

Deductions for food and accommodation, as well as repayment of registration fees, account for a large proportion of the deductions from nominal wages.[15] Even though wage rates are higher in Bangkok than in Mae Sot, workers report that deductions are also proportionately higher. In contrast no such deductions are made in Three Pagodas Pass as there is no pressure for workers to register officially. Some workers reported that in Mae Sot, the payment of accommodation costs takes the form of working extra shifts – commonly the 5–9 p.m. evening shift – in lieu of pay. The cost of obtaining a work permit as a temporary irregular migrant adds up to about 3,800 baht a year, and is commonly advanced by employers and deducted from wages over several months. But some workers reported that the workers who could not obtain a permit for whatever reason still have money deducted from their wages for a so-called 'immigration fee'. Employers tell them that this is to fund bail (or bribe) payments to get workers released if they are arrested, but it is widely believed that many employers levy this charge simply to cover the risk they believe they are taking by employing illegal migrants, though there is little evidence of any real risk of penalty in doing so. A number of workers reported that there was a further deduction of between 2 and 3 per cent of their earnings, and that either they were not aware of the reasons for deduction, or that it was to cover something called a 'landing fee', which was a term used by a number of migrant workers we interviewed, though it does not appear to correspond to any recognised category. The workers said it was a fee that they had to pay to agents to be allowed to work in the factories, above and beyond the charges they paid them to arrange their transportation and introduction.

Deductions are commonly made from workers' wages for making mistakes, for absences, for late starts. Recent research indicates that increasing levels of deduction meant that real wage levels in Mae Sot were lower in 2009 than in 2000.[16] This was also reflected in our interviews with workers, who claimed that they were better off in Three Pagodas Pass, because even though nominal wages were lower, they could actually earn more there than in Mae Sot, where they would be subject to high levels of deduction. A number of arbitrary and exorbitant charges result in a reduction of the actual amount paid in wages to migrant workers. According to San San Swe, who has been working in Mae Sot for the past six years:

> Migrants who want to start working in our factory need to give 1,500 baht to the manager to get a job in the sewing section. For the QC [quality control] or finishing sections, they have to pay 1,000 baht. Last month, five new workers started working here so she [the manager] got a lot of money... She has become rich by working in this factory. Also the workers who are late have to pay 20 baht a day, and if the workers forget to punch their timecard they also incur a 20 baht fine. If the workers have coffee, she deducts 100 baht – all these payments are deducted from the wages of the workers. She confiscates the phones of workers who are talking during working hours or who put their phones on the working desk; and many phones that are confiscated are not returned. In addition, the manager is organising

gambling inside the factory, particularly among the men, who are into football gambling. When the men lose money from gambling, she confiscates their ID cards, so she can then receive their wages directly – leaving some without any pay at the end of the month.

Even though there are no routine deductions for registration fees or accommodation in Three Pagodas Pass, it was reported that some employers routinely make deductions for reasons that are quite non-transparent, causing increased insecurity and uncertainty among the workers. Mu Mu Han, who had worked in Three Pagodas Pass for less than six months, was shocked by the unexpectedly high deductions:

> The employer deducted 2,000 baht for my agent fees and transportation costs. But the problem is that the manager also deducted other money from my wages [without telling me what it was for and how much]. So I did not have anything left on payday. In fact, the employer told me that he would deduct 500 baht so the debt would be finished after four months. But after working for four months I still owe about 1,000 baht.

The repayment of debts is a particular issue, given there is no security of employment for many migrant workers, as illustrated by the following account. Than Aye's sister introduced her to an agent who helped her to get to Thailand and find work in Three Pagodas Pass. But she says he did not make it clear that she would have to pay a fee for this service, and she ended up owing a considerable amount to her employer, who claimed to have paid the agent on her behalf.

> When I was in the old factory, I was a skilled machinist but there were no garments to sew. Now I sew 50–100 mosquito nets a day. This morning I was the first to come [to work]. I got up at 5 a.m. and I arrived at the factory at 6 a.m. I finished 50 mosquito nets this morning. But my income depends on the level of orders. Today we only had an order for 500 mosquito nets. By working here we can repay our debt as the employer will make deductions from our wages. This is fair but in the previous factory I worked in [the employer] continued to make deductions even when we were not

earning, so our debt just increased. How can we repay our debt if they deduct when we are not earning? We have no pay left, and we have to borrow to survive, which means we accumulate more and more debt.

Migrant workers' relatively low earnings are barely enough to cover their daily living costs, with any surplus used to support their families at home, leaving little to save for any contingencies, such as unexpected health-care charges. Many workers are constantly in debt. Kaythi Min Soe, a Burman Muslim, came to Mae Sot from Yangon leaving her three children with her mother-in-law. Her husband works in Bangkok and she is determined to save enough money to build a house in two years. But, as she explains below, it is difficult to save money because her monthly earnings can completely disappear on payday due to all her commitments:

We only have one day off a month. When I have a holiday, I have to wash, clean and cook. I even don't have time to go out. [But] today I went to the market to buy clothes for my daughter. Yesterday I received my pay of 2,200 baht. I repaid what I had borrowed last month from my sister [to send to my children 50,000 k (1,500 Thai baht)]. Then I gave 500 baht to my sister, who cooks for me, for food for the whole month. Then I am left with 200 baht in my hand. I bought one skirt for my daughter to wear in Burma that cost 170 baht. Now I don't have any money. In my factory, we receive 300 baht for living outside the factory [as housing allowance] if we don't take leave for a whole month.

However, some women did report that they have been able to save something from their wages. Saving money in a safe place is a challenge for migrant workers; most do not have bank accounts – there is widespread mistrust of banks, so generally they keep their money in their rooms. Some women confided that they had purchased gold jewellery, though they are afraid to wear it in Thailand because this can lead to undesirable attention from others, particularly the local population and the Thai police. One such woman is Sandar Aye, who had been working in Mae Sot for seven years. Her parents had died many years previously, so she remitted money to her older sister until she got married. Now that she has a child, she keeps her savings in Thailand:

> When I have about 3,000 baht in my hands, I buy one piece of gold. I don't want to keep money [cash] in my hands, and I don't remit to Burma because I don't have my parents in Burma to save money for me. It is good to save in gold because when I need money I can go and sell it. But I never wear these pieces of gold because you know this is not my country and if something happens to us, we will lose them. I prefer to wear the gold in my country. Here, I don't want to get attention from Thai people by wearing them. I prefer Thai people to think of me as poor so that they will feel pity for me.

We heard accounts of workers who lent money with interest to their friends, or who sent lump sums home to invest in relatives' businesses. But the general vulnerability and insecurity in which migrant workers live in Thailand makes it difficult for them to protect themselves against contingencies, or to explore alternative opportunities for themselves.

Safety, security and harassment, deportation

When migrant workers without the required documentation are apprehended by police in Thailand, they will be detained and deported to Burma unless the employer intervenes and pays what is called a fine. This happens more frequently to those who are working in Mae Sot, and many report that they have experienced multiple detentions and deportations, but are able to re-cross the border without difficulty. However, there seems to be little police activity in Three Pagodas Pass, and the question of deporting daily commuting workers does not arise. But the workers were of the view that if they tried to travel further inland they would encounter problems with the authorities. In the central provinces there are frequent media reports of police raids and deportations, though the workers we spoke to had not been subject to arrest and deportation.

Workers in Mae Sot, however, live with a daily fear of detention; over 40 per cent of our sample had experienced deportation. The figures were higher for male workers, over half of whom had been deported, mainly because of men's more visible presence on the streets, particularly at night. According to an officer interviewed at Mae Sot police station, the Tak Immigration Office deports around 300 Burmese workers per day, handing them over to the Burmese military at the border.

Although few migrants in Bangkok and Three Pagodas Pass have been arrested or deported, many have had to take action to escape the attentions of the police, particularly when they have attempted to travel any distance from their workplace. In Bangkok, police raids on factories generally follow a tip-off from an informer; one such incident followed a dispute between Burmese migrant workers and Thai workers employed at a neighbouring factory, and resulted in the deportation of the migrant workers. In Mae Sot factory raids on illegal immigrants by police are usually linked to inspection visits by the immigration police from Bangkok. Although, as we reported earlier, local police are frequently informed of an immigrant raid by their colleagues; if they inform the factory management, the workers can flee to the other side of the river until the inspection is over. Although there have been no police raids in Three Pagodas Pass itself, workers interviewed there had heard of an incident in the provincial town of Kanchanaburi where migrant workers panicked when the police came to the factory, and tried to escape by climbing over a wall, resulting in several workers drowning in the river.

Workers in Bangkok also reported aggressive behaviour by the police who conduct raids on the accommodation used by migrant workers. They explained that when the police come, they search the building one room at a time. Workers therefore try to keep quiet so the police do not find them. However, the police apply an electric current to the floor to force them to reveal their whereabouts. But the migrants keep a plastic sheet spread out on the floor, which they said helps protect them from the electric shock. Without such protection the migrants would shout out and reveal their presence. Migrant workers in Mae Sot have been known to flee to the surrounding jungle areas in order to escape police raids on accommodation areas.

More than half the workers interviewed in Bangkok and Mae Sot reported that they had to pay off police who detained them in order to secure their release. These sums can be quite high – the going rate in Bangkok was reported to be 2,500 baht and although the bribes were lower in Mae Sot, with an average of 130 baht being reported, workers there are caught more frequently; over 20 per cent of our all respondents in Mae Sot, and over 30 per cent of the men, had paid off the police more than three times. In Three Pagodas Pass, workers told us that they only had to pay police when they ventured out of the town, which was an infrequent occurrence.

The high pay-offs demanded by police in Bangkok are a further incentive for migrants in the central provinces to register, even though the financial cost of doing so is high. There is more reluctance in Mae Sot and Three Pagodas Pass, especially among women, who are less willing to go to the trouble and expense of obtaining legal documentation. Sandar Aye had been unable to continue working in the factory after the birth of her child, but now worked as an outworker at home, receiving work from the factories:

> I don't need an ID card because I don't go out anywhere. My husband has an ID card, which he needs for his job. It is very costly [to pay for registration] for both of us. The expense is 4,000 baht each. I can save that amount by not registering.

The reluctance of women to bear the expense of registration reflects the fact that they tend to earn less than men, but also points to their restricted mobility. Kaythi Min Soe's husband is working in Bangkok, but she has decided to stay in Mae Sot even though the wages are lower, since it is easier to cross back into Burma should something happen to her children:

> If we obtain ID cards, we need to spend a lot. For me it is not possible [to register and get ID card] because I only earn 84 baht a day. If I do get an ID card, I will be deducted 850 baht for the first two months, and 500 baht a month the following months. In the

following year, the deductions would be a bit less – about 300 baht a month. But it is still a lot of money for me compared with what I earn. That is why I don't register. And I don't need to go outside [the factory compound]. We can avoid the police.

Those involved in policing the migrant workers in Thailand are well aware of the contradictions of the policies they have to implement. A police spokesman interviewed at Mae Sot police station was of the opinion that arrest and deportation are not cost-effective, since this action does not discourage migrant workers from coming to Thailand.

> The normal criminal punishments do not apply to migrants and are not effective in restricting their numbers. If we catch them and send them back home, they will come back. If we catch them and re-educate them, it is no use, since they are not criminals, and they would anyway go back home [to Burma] in the future. So, whatever we are now doing against migrants is a waste of tax money. (Mae Sot Police Station)

It would seem that the new registration procedures are less accessible for women workers, particularly those who are resident within a factory compound, and have restricted mobility or little interaction with the local community. The cost of legalising migrant workers' status is now substantially higher than the previous arrangements, which is a real disincentive to women who earn lower wages and have a longer and ongoing commitment to send money to their families at home and to support any children they may have. But without regularising their situation they remain vulnerable to arbitrary and punitive treatment from immigration and police authorities, all of which contributes to their convenience for employers, who require a cheap and flexible workforce.

Relations with friends

The working and living conditions of migrant factory workers in Thailand are hard, and many live under constant fear of deportation. They have little protection from the law and few possibilities to negotiate any improvements in their lives. For that reason, support from friends and relatives with knowledge and contacts in Thailand is central to their survival strategy, supplying them with intelligence about job vacancies, contacts with agents and managers, temporary accommodation and food and credit to tide them over until they can establish themselves independently. Migrants also look to their compatriots to provide them with psychological support, to help them familiarise themselves with the rules and structures in Thailand, and to reduce the sense of isolation and marginalisation they experience as a consequence of leaving their families and familiar surroundings. Mu Mu Han's friendship networks, which comprise both kin and co-workers in Three Pagodas Pass, provided an important source of support for her:

> When I have some free time I go to visit my friends on both sides of the border and [I also visit] my mother's friend's son, who brought me here. Whenever I visit them, they give me food, and I can have rice anywhere I go. I don't need to worry about food. Here in this present factory, my friends are good. They also help me – for example they taught me how to sew up trousers. In the old branch [of the factory where I used to work], the manager's wife was very bad-tempered, and whenever I asked about the sewing style she was not patient and shouted at me.

Visiting friends is the main leisure activity of most women workers, but also a necessary survival strategy. The connections with people who come from the same place of origin are an important feature of this strategy, which is true of migrant workers in many different situations.

In lieu of their original families and networks, migrant workers create new communities often based on mutual cooperation at work, but extending to activities and support in many areas of their lives. Because of the long working days most women do not have much time to interact with each other, let alone go out of the factory and socialize with people. However, they do have a strong sense of community:

We [my friends, sister and husband] eat together but we cook separately. Most of the time we work in the factory, so we don't have much time to go out or spend time with other friends. Last week there was a funeral in our factory. That worker was quite old and she died of cancer. She had stopped working when she got ill but had worked here for three years. But we organised a funeral for her since her husband still works at this factory. We collected money to pay for the funeral. The owner contributed 10,000 baht for her funeral... and gave us a three-hour break to attend the ceremony... If someone gets married we have a marriage ceremony in the factory. Sometimes if we want to go to the temple and hear the Buddhist monk preach we take time off from the factory and go together. (San San Swe of Mae Sot)

Such linkages with fellow Burmese workers are important, especially because most of them do not understand the Thai language and can be easy prey for Thais who want to take advantage of their vulnerability. Htet Htet Hlaing used to work at the border area of Ranong, and through an agent came to Bangkok with her husband. But work was irregular and they constantly had to look for new jobs. Such insecurity made her a prey for ill-meaning Thais who took advantage of her:

We were jobless for many days. We were cheated by a Thai who was our neighbour because we did not have any jobs and we did not speak Thai. One day when my husband went outside, a Thai man came to my room and told me that my husband was working in a particular place. I also need to go there to work. I could not understand him but he told me to come along with him so I did. He took me to a village where he sold me to a Thai woman... I fled the village. I did not know where to go. I decided to go back to Burma since I had 5,000 baht in my hands. I did not know where my husband was... I told the agent to take me back to Burma.

Migrant workers' survival networks extend beyond their fellow factory workers, and include agents who organise job placements, remittances and so on. Thin Thin Myint, a Burman woman who migrated to Mae Sot after working for some years in a garment factory in Yangon, relies on the agent who organised her journey for a range of services:

[The agent] is about 35 years old, and has a family in Yangon... we have known each other since we worked together in a factory there. She [the agent] has been coming to Mae Sot for more than five years and she knew this factory owner very well. She used to recruit workers for this factory. She goes back to Yangon once a month and brings back new workers and she also takes money and goods to give to our parents. When she comes to Mae Sot she stays in the factory accommodation with us and sells food to workers. She cooks curries and sells to workers on credit. She has a good business here. In addition, whenever she goes back she buys goods from Mae Sot to sell in Yangon.

Sometimes migrant workers in Thailand, who are already struggling with the challenges of work and survival, find it difficult to deal with the burden of taking responsibility for recently arrived friends and relatives. Marlar Kyaw came to Three Pagodas Pass two years ago. She is an unmarried woman in her mid-thirties, who worked in a garment factory in Yangon for ten years. She is a skilled machinist but her income is irregular, sometimes due to lack of orders and sometimes because there is no electricity in the factory. She remits to her aunt back home. Even though she does not have any children or other family to support, she is worried about taking on the responsibility of looking after relatives who want to join her in Three Pagodas Pass, though she is exploring ways to help them:

They [my cousins] want to come [to Thailand to work] but the responsibility for a person [to arrange for their stay] is too big [for me] to accept. I have to think carefully because if my cousins don't listen to me I will have problems here. It is very far from our home town and we have to make decisions by ourselves whatever we do. We have to look after ourselves well. There are many bad things here like gambling, lottery – [it is a] dangerous life if we cannot control ourselves. By bringing my relatives, I will be taking all their problems upon myself... But I want to have my relatives here so I can spend time with them and talk to them.

In some cases, migrants have to dissuade their relatives from joining them, because the costs and risks are too great. Khin Myat

Aye came to Three Pagodas Pass three and a half years ago when she was 40 years old. Her father and brothers did not approve of her marriage and she was initially disowned, but later was reconciled with her family. However, there was a family conflict about her father's will so she came to work in Three Pagodas Pass. Her youngest brother was the only one in the family who approved of her decision so she wanted to help him by bringing him and his family to Three Pagodas Pass:

> I thought that if I can earn well here I want my youngest brother's family to come here because they are poor in Burma. But when I think about looking for jobs for them – sending [their] three children to school here and feeding the whole family until they find work – it is not possible. I myself would not be able to survive by helping them. That is why I can't help them at the moment.

The lives of migrant factory workers in Thailand are stressful and precarious and they live under constant fear – of unemployment, of indebtedness, of arrest, deportation and failure. However, in spite of their low wages, and their powerless in the face of unfair practices and deductions and fines, they are struggling to forge a life for themselves and their families. A particular concern for women workers is the challenge of maintaining their roles as workers and wage earners, and dealing with the responsibilities of becoming wives and mothers as well as their ongoing obligations towards their families back home.

5

Burmese migrant women and families in Thailand: reproduction, children and care

For the growing number of Burmese migrants who are mothers as well as workers, a major challenge is accessing appropriate maternity services; another is how to finance and organise the care of their children while continuing to work in the export factories. These are women who in general have very limited knowledge of the Thai language, who are away from their familiar sources of support and assistance, and who in many cases have very little experience of using health or other services in the location where they work. Many are facing maternity for the first time, often in relatively unstable relationships with partners they have met since their migration to Thailand. They are living in a situation where the state is explicitly hostile to migrant women having children within its territory; they get no protection from the law in terms of maternity rights or pension, and employers generally regard them as a problem. But the migrant women we encountered in Thailand exhibited remarkable versatility in the ways in which they responded to these challenges, calling on a range of resources and institutions including family, community and religious networks to help meet their needs. Needless to say, the arrangements they were able to make are not necessarily ideal from an outside perspective, nor conducive to family stability or child welfare networks.

Structural analyses of migrant workers tend to focus either on their contribution to economic growth and accumulation in different contexts, or on the discrimination and exploitation they experience in situations where they have minimal rights and protection. There is less interest in considering migrant workers as real human beings, with the same kind of aspirations and expectations as non-migrant individuals. This is especially true with respect to the life-cycle experience of migrant workers; whilst numerous accounts of migrants working in garments and textiles not just in Thailand but all over the world highlight the female-intense nature of such employment, and report the employment of women in the 15 to 25 age group, it is surprising how little attention has been given to the fact that these workers are in their prime reproductive years.

Pregnancy and childbirth

The Burmese women who are the focus of our study mainly come to Thailand as single women, though a good number arrive as part of a couple or a family group. More than half the women (57.1 per cent) reported that they had given birth to their first child since their migration to Thailand. This is especially true of the workforce in Mae Sot; many of the workers in Bangkok and neighbouring provinces tended to be older when they arrived and had already had children.

Decisions about how to organise their reproductive responsibilities start as soon as they become pregnant. The question of where to deliver the baby preoccupies all migrant prospective mothers. In theory, they have a choice between continuing with their pregnancy in their place of employment in Thailand or returning to Burma, generally to their home town or village, to deliver the baby there. The decision is complicated and they need to consider a range of factors, including the cost of the delivery in each location, the

TABLE 5.1　Country of birth of first child by respondent's location

	Bangkok	Mae Sot	Three Pagoda Pass	Total
Born after coming to Thailand	37 (37.4%)	207 (70.2%)	39 (38.2%)	283 (57.1%)
Born before coming to Thailand	62 (62.6%)	88 (29.8%)	63 (61.8%)	213 (42.9%)
Total	99 (100%)	295 (100%)	102 (100%)	496 (100%)

Source Questionnaire survey 2010.

cost of travelling back home, the implications for their ability to retain their job or return to work after the pregnancy, and the resources and support they will need both during the pregnancy confinement and afterwards.

Migrant workers in Thailand need to make pragmatic decisions about pregnancy and childbirth. It is clear from our research that workers already resident and employed in factories in the centre of the country around Bangkok were least likely to return to Burma to have their children. This bears out our earlier assessment that by the time such women were settled and employed in Bangkok they were more likely to have some kind of documentation, and to be better settled in Thailand. They were less willing to commit the time and expense involved in returning home, and were fearful of the risk such a journey might entail, particularly since the return journey is long and frequently hazardous.

The situation is different in the border locations of Mae Sot and Three Pagodas Pass, where travel between Burma and Thailand makes childbirth in Burma a feasible option for migrant women. Some 86 per cent of our sample in Mae Sot reported that they had opted to have their babies in Mae Sot rather than return to their homes in Burma. Their choice reflected the lower cost of maternity and childbirth in Mae Sot. Registered migrant workers can access maternity care in the government hospital for the standard charge of 30 baht, although the total cost of pregnancy and childbirth care would be very much higher. Even non-registered migrants have access to good and low-cost services in the Mae Tao Clinic, which is run by Magsaysay award winner Dr Cynthia Maung. The facilities in Mae Sot were reported to be far superior to what was on offer in their native Burma. Aye Aye Khin is a Mon from Pa-an in her late twenties, who has been working in Mae Sot for five years:

> Mae Sot hospital has modern machines and equipment to deliver the baby. In my home town the electricity is not regular and we have to pay for generator charges and [there is] no modern machinery and equipment. It is safer to deliver in Mae Sot than at home.

In Three Pagodas Pass workers tend to use the hospital on the Burmese side of the border in preference to the small public health centre which is all that is available on the Thai side. Since most workers commute without any ID card or Thai documentation they are unable to access the better hospital facilities in the district centre of Sangklaburi. Many women therefore give birth in Three Pagodas Pass on the Burmese side or return to their home town, although the fact that the road from other parts of Burma to Three Pagodas Pass is very rough and therefore unsuitable for pregnant women in the latter stages of their pregnancies can deter them from making this journey.

The decision hinges not just on the cost of care for the pregnancy and birth but also the implications for the worker in terms of maintaining her employment as well as the care of the child in the longer run. The experience of San Htun, who came to Samut Prakan four years ago with her husband, is typical. They tried to get jobs in a factory which supports the registration of its workers, but were not successful. Her husband frequently changed jobs in search of higher wages, but San Htun preferred to stay in familiar surroundings, doubting that the working conditions would be any different elsewhere. When she got pregnant, she went for antenatal care in a private clinic, which was costly.

> To deliver the baby here is very expensive since we don't have ID cards. So we [my husband and me] decided to go back to Burma to deliver the baby there with our parents – there is no one who can take care of the baby here. If I deliver the child here, my husband has to take leave from his job at the same time as I am not working. So it is pointless to deliver the baby here when neither of us is working.

In the end, San Htun's husband decided to stay in Bangkok and let San Htun go back to Burma alone, because he wanted to stay with his current employer, who had paid for his medical costs following an injury he sustained at work.

Although most women plan to work through their pregnancies, health problems can make this difficult. Phyu Tun came to Three Pagodas Pass three years ago with her brother and sisters when she was 27 years old. She got married within a year and the following year became pregnant.

> We have worked at three different mosquito net factories. At first we were not experienced so we earned less, but when we became skilled we could earn more and even save some money. However, after three or four months of having a good level of wages, I got pregnant... I could not work hard because of morning sickness.

In some cases, employers were unwilling to allow pregnant women to continue working, which can leave the worker in a very difficult situation. May Hnin Khaing had worked in Thailand for thirteen years before she got pregnant at the age of 35 while employed in a factory near Bangkok:

> I was dizzy and felt faint when I got pregnant... I did not want to stop working but the boss said it would be a problem if I fell down and injured my head, or if I had a miscarriage, which could create problems for the factory owner... That is why I had to leave the job. I did not have any right to paid sick leave although I was registered.

She went back to Burma to give birth. However, her mother died shortly after the birth and in the absence of any other family childcare options she returned to Thailand with the child.

If women are unable to continue working due to pregnancy, families often have to take out further loans, increasing their already high levels of debt. Sabeh Han came to Bangkok when she was 26 years old and got married three years later. She got into debt because she spent a lot of money on her marriage ceremony, and also on a trip back home when her mother was ill. But because of the pregnancy she could not meet the repayment schedule:

> When I got pregnant, I stopped working in the fish canning factory where I had worked for four years. While I was pregnant my health prevented me from earning a steady income and I still have debt of 10,000 baht from the loan I took out. At the time I thought I could repay my debt in a few months but with an interest rate of 15 per cent I still have not finished paying it back after nearly a year.

Another worker reported that she was sacked when the manager discovered that she was pregnant, because the owner believed that employing pregnant women would bring bad luck. Nearly a fifth of the women we interviewed who had had their first child after arriving in Thailand had left their jobs during their pregnancies for one reason or another.

The difficulties of sustaining a pregnancy while seeking to maintain their employment, as well as the worry about the cost of care for mother and child, contributes to the significant number of migrant workers who terminate their pregnancies. Hun Su Mynt, a garment worker in Samut Prakhan, told us that

> My husband's younger brother, who is also working in Thailand, was not able to send any money to his mother after he got married. When his wife got pregnant she had to have an abortion as they couldn't afford to deliver the baby.

According to Dr Cynthia Maung,[1] 55 per cent of maternal mortality among Burmese women at her Mae Tao clinic is caused by post-abortion complications; of the fourteen pregnant women who died at the Tak public hospital in 2001-02 none was Thai.

Some women choose to postpone or avoid pregnancy, using contraceptives supplied by local drug stores and medical centres.

We understand that contraceptive education and availability is limited in Burma, partly because of the government's pro-natalist policy and partly because of the relatively low level of expenditure on health services, particularly community services and preventative medicine.[2]

A key factor in the decision to continue with a pregnancy or not, and if so to give birth in Thailand or Burma, is whether the worker is registered and has the appropriate documentation. Moe Moe Htun has been working in Samut Prakhan for two years. At first she worked with her husband running a fishing enterprise in Burma, but after their business collapsed they sold up and came to Thailand, leaving their two children with her husband's mother:

> Since most of the workers do not have ID cards, it is difficult for women to be pregnant and deliver a baby here. It is expensive for a woman without an ID card to deliver a baby... We have to do like this [*gestures*] [to get a contraceptive injection], otherwise, once you get pregnant and [have no] ID card, you'd better go home. It costs 2,000 baht to go back over the border. We can't afford to get pregnant.

There has been a concerted international campaign against the use of Depo-Provera and other injectable contraceptives because of fears about the long-term effect on women's health and fertility. However, for many migrant women in Thailand this was the only contraceptive available to them. Thet Htar Lwin is a 28-year-old, who came to Three Pagodas Pass with her new husband just seven months prior to the interview. She has found work in a garment factory.

> I have no money to have a child now. I am taking contraceptive injections every three months at this clinic. I am still struggling for survival – when I have a permanent place to stay, and have enough money to eat and some extra money then I want to have a child.

The regulatory system for migrant workers is essentially one of facilitating the temporary employment of low-paid workers, who are only legally permitted to remain in the country in order to sell their labour power, often at illegally low rates, to Thai employers, who are competing in local and international markets on the basis of low cost. There is no consideration of the rights of workers to have children and a normal family life; indeed the increasingly restrictive regulation of irregular migrants explicitly restricts the reproductive rights of the workers employed. The hostility of the Thai government to the possibility of migrant workers having children has been frequently aired, and, as is discussed in Chapter 6, has been used to mobilise Thai public opinion against migrants during the recent economic crisis. But such hostility is long-standing. General Sonthi Boonyaratglin, former deputy prime minister in charge of national security, reacted strongly to the news that 2,000 babies were born each month to foreign migrant workers in Mahachai in Samut Sakorn province. He advocated the compulsory return of pregnant foreign migrant women, many of whom moved from Samut Sakorn to the neighbouring Samut Prakarn province to avoid arrest.[3]

The question of the child's nationality also has a bearing on the decision of where to give birth. As discussed in Chapter 4, children born to migrant mothers do not acquire Thai nationality and generally do not have any official birth certificates or nationality documents. Moreover they are only entitled to Burmese nationality if they are born and registered in Burma. The local midwife has to report to the appropriate government office to certify that the baby was born in Burma and thus registers the child as Burmese. This must be done within a year and a half of the child's birth. This is not considered to be a difficult procedure for the migrants, and registration frequently takes place in their absence, though this is not possible for those who do not return or do not have relatives who can help them. But many women migrants, especially those from conflict areas, do not themselves possess any kind of Burmese ID card, which means they are effectively excluded from the systems of regulation in both Burma and Thailand. Most migrants in this situation are not aware of their rights and entitlements or of the implications of non-registration for themselves and their children.

Childcare

Questions of citizenship as well as practical questions of time, money and resources are also central to decisions about where to raise and educate children born to migrant workers. With estimates of over 500,000 stateless children already living in Thailand, with numbers growing year on year, this is an issue that is assuming greater significance, and needs to be resolved at policy level as well as at the individual family level.

The factory workers in the three locations where we carried out our research have adopted various strategies to secure the care of their children. Slightly more than half of these children currently live in Burma, with the children of migrants in the central provinces being more likely to be living with their relatives back home than with their parents. The pattern in Three Pagodas Pass is more complex: 57 per cent of the children of migrant factory workers lived with relatives inside Burma, whilst the rest lived with their mothers, generally staying on the Burmese side of the border from where their mothers commute to work.

An important finding from the research is the complex ways in which these women have constantly to change their childcare arrangements, depending on what support they can access on both sides of the border. Table 5.2 summarises the patterns of care in place for children of migrant workers in the three locations. The situation in Three Pagodas Pass would seem to be most straightforward: only 8 of the 39 women who were involved in the survey had actually sent their children back to their home towns or villages in Burma, and 5 of those had kept the child with them when they were a small infant. The overwhelming majority lived in the burgeoning settlements on the Burmese side of the border, where there are a number of elementary schools which have grown up especially to cater for the children of migrant workers; there are boarding facilities for the children of migrants who find employment in the factories around Bangkok. Workers in Mae Sot appear to have more flexibility, particularly in terms of support

TABLE 5.2 Childcare patterns for children under 6 years old for those respondents who delivered a child after coming to Thailand, by location[4]

	Bangkok	Mae Sot	Three Pagodas Pass[5]	Total
Childcare by oneself in Thailand	10 (27.0%)	19 (9.2%)	29 (74.4%)	58 (20.5%)
Childcare by paid caretaker in Thailand	2 (5.4%)	18 (8.7%)	0 (0%)	20 (7.1%)
Childcare by oneself in Thailand then send child to Burma	20 (54.1%)	78 (37.7%)	5 (12.8%)	103 (36.4%)
Childcare by oneself in Thailand then invite parents to Thailand	3 (8.1%)	96 (46.4%)	14 (35.9%)	113 (39.9%)
Childcare in Burma	2 (5.4%)	31 (15.0%)	3 (7.7%)	36 (12.7%)
Total	37 (100%)	207 (100%)	39 (100%)	283 (100%)

Source Questionnaire survey 2010.

from parents and other family members who are able to travel relatively freely from their homes to Myawaddy (on the Burmese side of the river border) or Mae Sot to help care for small children whilst their parents are working. This is not possible for workers in Bangkok because the distance from the border and the high level of surveillance of migrants preclude unregistered family members from joining working mothers to share the burden of childcare.

It would seem that a common pattern for workers in both Mae Sot and Bangkok is to keep the children with them in their early years and then to send them back to live with relatives when they are older. However, our research indicates that many women found it necessary to make frequent changes to the arrangements, juggling between keeping their children with them in Thailand and sending them to their families in Burma. Twelve respondents in Mae Sot have changed their childcare arrangement three times before the child was 6 years old, shifting the infant across the border, and several respondents in the other locations reported changing childcare arrangements twice during the child's early years. Table 5.2 summarises the arrangements made by migrant factory workers concerning the care of small children.

Decisions about childcare arrangements depend not just on relative cost and convenience, but also on what care options are offered by family members. In some cases mothers and mothers-in-law are already caring for the children of other siblings and are not able to take on any more. Kaythi Min Soe, a garment worker in Mae Sot, said that her mother in-law in Burma was looking after seven children between the ages of 2 and 15 years old: three of her children and the children of two of her sisters. The other sisters were able to send substantial remittances home from their jobs in Malaysia and China respectively, which meant that the grandmother had sufficient resources to care for all the children. However, other workers are not able to rely on the same level of support and many were worried that their families did not have sufficient funds to feed and care for the children they had sent back home, particularly if there was no other income going into the household. Lynn Myat Aung and her husband have been working in Samut Prakan since 2004, leaving her two children under the care of her mother-in-law. However, when their income became less stable they found it difficult to maintain their remittances. At the same time, her sister-in-law died, leaving three children to be cared for by the mother-in-law, who faced a falling level of funds and an increased care load. So now the children are cared for by her own mother, though their unreliable earnings and remittances make Lynn Myat Aung afraid of what might happen in the future.

In some cases an additional child means that carefully constructed networks of support are no longer sufficient, forcing some workers to change employer in order to be able to continue working. When Soe Soe Aung, a worker in a knitting factory in

Mae Sot, had her first child, her mother, who was living in Mae Sot at the time, was able to look after the baby in addition to caring for three other grandchildren. But when her second child was born she felt another baby would be too much for her mother, so she had to leave her job in order to look after the children, leaving the family dependent on her husband's low wage. She did the occasional casual labouring work on days when her mother was able to look after the children, but it all got too much for her mother, who decided to return to Burma with the five grandchildren, where other relatives could help with the childcare. Soe Soe Aung was then available for full-time work but was not able to earn enough to send sufficient money to her mother, who was taking care of her two young children, so she decided to bring the children back to Mae Sot. But without childcare she could not continue working in the factory, so she took on some subcontracted home-based work which paid much less. At the time of our interview she had concluded that she could not make ends meet and intended to send her children back to Burma so she would be free to go to Bangkok to find a better-paying job.

In general the options seem wider for those in Mae Sot, a well-established border town with a range of Burmese community services including schools and health-care clinics as well as temples, migrant workers' organisations and, to some extent, a tradition of community solidarity and self-help. For these reasons many migrant workers were content to stay working in this town in spite of the lower wages and endless harassment from factory owners, managers, police and immigration authorities.

New mothers frequently have to rely on help from their parents even in situations when they have migrated against their parents' wishes. But, as May Thin Aye discovered, this is often an expensive option. She had come to Mae Sot in 2004 with her sisters and in 2006 she got married and became pregnant. Her father did not approve of her marriage, since her husband was an ethnic Chin while she was a Burman. But because of her problems her parents came to Myawaddy to look after the infant:

When my baby was about two months old I had to return to work, so I asked my parents to help me take care of my baby. They came and stayed in Myawaddy for about one and a half months, so I left the baby with my parents while I stayed in the factory compound to work. I would visit my daughter and my parents at the weekends when I had time off. But it all got very expensive; I had to pay for the transport to Myawaddy every weekend and my parents had to renew their Myawaddy residence permit weekly, which cost 1,000 kyats per person.

Su Su Win in Mae Sot had to return to work three months after her confinement, or she would have lost her job. She told us that she hired a child-minder, which cost 1,000 baht a month (almost a quarter of her earnings). But she had to move back into the factory hostel, which was cheaper than living outside. This meant that she could only see her baby during weekends. When the factory went on short time through lack of orders, she could no longer afford to pay the child-minder, so she arranged for a pregnant neighbour to care for the child without pay, no doubt in anticipation of support when her own child was born.

The situation in Three Pagodas Pass is very different. The recent growth of factories, which has attracted thousands of migrant workers, has resulted in a town that appears to be a virtual Burmese settlement, in spite of it being under Thai jurisdiction. The workers are housed in shanty-town-like houses on the Burmese side of the border, which is marked only by a low wire fence. Many workers reported that they had found no difficulty in finding local (Burmese) women to look after small children if their own family was not able to provide care for them. According to Lwin Maw Tun, 'There are many neighbours who are free and could look after the baby for a while during the day.'

When Burmese migrant workers do decide to send their children back to Burma they are influenced by notions of national identity and culture as well as economic rationales or concern for the well-being of the child. The interview below with a married couple working in one of the Bangkok factories indicates the different perspectives and pressures women face when deciding how best to arrange care for their children born in Thailand. Yee Nwe Hlaing is a Karen-Pa-O in her mid-thirties and her Pa-O husband has been working in Thailand for over ten years. They have two school-aged children in Burma and are now thinking of sending their five-month-old baby back to Burma to be looked after by Hlaing's mother:

> *Interviewer* Are you going to send [the child] back soon?
>
> *Husband* Currently we have someone to take care of him. In the future my wife might get fired and I might lose my job after that, then both of us will be jobless. Nowadays the factories are very strict.
>
> *Wife* No sister. This is not the reason. This environment here is very dirty. We don't want to keep the baby [here] because it is dangerous for the baby. The doctor said that... [there is] pollution from nearby factories – the air is not clean and the ground is very greasy because of the waste from the factories. [So it isn't] good for young children and babies.

Sandar Aye reported that she had wanted to send her son back to her mother-in-law in Burma and then move from Mae Sot to Bangkok, in response to ongoing active recruitment initiatives by factory managers from Bangkok. But her 3-year-old son kept getting sick every time she left him with the family in Burma:

> When I intended to go to Bangkok, my son was ill in Burma so we had to go and pick him up. While he is here [in Mae Sot] with us, I could not go to Bangkok. The second time, the employer from Bangkok came [to take us to work in Bangkok], but I could not send my son back to my mother-in-law [in Burma] because when I planned to leave him, he got sick, so my husband did not let me go and work in Bangkok. I don't have *zartar* [luck] to go to Bangkok.

Sandar Aye's husband is a Karen, though she herself is Burman. Some parents, particularly fathers, have strong views about the importance of reproducing their children's ethnic identity, and insist on sending their children to their natal families, even against the wishes of their wives.

My husband does not want to send the child to nursery [in Mae Sot].
He would like to send him to his hometown to be with his mother
and learn Karen and Burmese... my husband does not like the
learning and teaching system here. He has very high expectations
for his son. He is our firstborn, and my husband thinks he needs
to have a good education, because when he grows up he needs to
be the head of the family. His side of the family is well educated
– unlike my family who don't have much education. Both his
brothers and sister passed grade 10, he passed grade 7. So he wants
to keep his son with his family, rather than with mine, and raise
him as a Karen. His mother calls us and insists on speaking to her
grandson in Karen so as to maintain the Karen culture. My son
learnt to speak Karen very well while he was with his grandmother,
though he has forgotten a lot of it now... I have to respect my
husband's wishes... If the child was a daughter it would be no
problem. You know, being a girl, she does not have to be educated
– she will not have to be head of the family so would not need to
stay with her father's family and be educated. That is why I want to
have another child, a daughter, then I could keep her with me and
not worry about her education.

If workers do decide to send their infants back to their families in
Burma, there are practical problems about how to get them there.
This is particularly acute for those who live in the provinces near
to Bangkok. The journey back to Burma with a baby is relatively
straightforward, but if the mother wants to come back to the work
in Bangkok the return trip is more hazardous and less secure. We
met a Nepalese-Burman couple in Samut Prakan who had decided
to send their three-month-old baby back home so that the wife,
Chaw Su Yee, could continue working in Bangkok. But she was
very fearful of the journey.

I need to take the baby back to Burma, but whenever I think about
the return trip from Burma I get upset. My journey to come here was
bad enough. I walked for three days and when we got on the truck it
was really overcrowded. I don't want to go through such a trip again.
I've never gone back to Burma since I came here three years. To go
back with the baby is quite easy; we don't need to spend much money
and the trip is smooth, just to take the bus from Bangkok to Mae Sot

and cross over. But to come back is difficult. Yet I have no choice
– no one can come here to look after my baby because staying in
Bangkok without documents is impossible

Because of the difficulties women working in the central provinces face in travelling to and from their homes inside Burma to
deliver their babies or take them back to be cared for by their
families so they can return to work, there is now a demand for a new
kind of middleman – a 'baby agent' who, at a price, will organise
the transportation of babies and children from Bangkok to the
workers' home towns and villages inside Burma. We were told that
these agents transport several babies in one trip, usually drugging
them to prevent them crying on the journey. One woman told us
she had arranged with one such agent to take her young baby back
to Burma, but was so dismayed when she saw the number of babies
that were going on the journey with only one or two adult carers
responsible for their health and well-being that she changed her
mind and decided to take her child back herself. However, recently
the practice of taking several infants at a time has ceased because
the strict checks relating to anti-human-trafficking agreements
and practices have made it too risky, so baby agents are now only
able to take one child at a time.

If the migrant workers do decide to keep their children in
Thailand, there are several possible childcare options, depending
on their networks and resources, and also the particular situation
of their employment. Those working in Three Pagodas Pass and
in some small factories in Mae Sot, where the factory regime is
relatively relaxed, were frequently able to bring their small children
to the workplace. May Thin Aye, a young mother working in Mae
Sot, recalled that she was able to have the baby in a cradle next
to the machine at which she was working so she could breastfeed
her baby at work.

> The factory I was working at that time had a quite flexible work
> environment; it was quite close to my house, and they [the employer]
> would allow me to go back and see my baby when she cried.

This is not an ideal solution, however, as it is hard to concentrate on sewing with a baby needing attention, and it can mean a serious drop in earnings, especially for those working on piece rates; so most women have to make different arrangements as the child gets older and more active. If there is no family nearby who can help, some mothers are able to hire other Burmese women who live locally, an option that is made possible by the extensive long-established migrant communities in Mae Sot and other areas. Often older women who cannot get employment in the factories are willing to work as childminders, though this can cost up to half of the mother's income.

Not all workplaces are child-friendly, and the situation can depend on the capriciousness of particular managers; in one case in Mae Sot a new factory owner revoked the previous practice of allowing young children to stay in factory accommodation and instituted a fine of 900 baht if women brought their infants to work. This is one of the reasons why women are forced to change job even though the official registration regulations make this difficult.

Hiring others to care for small children can also be problematic, as the rules concerning accommodation make it impossible to organise informal arrangements for a childminder to look after a group of children. Even when there is a nursery, because of the rules in the factory and the working requirement of the workers, it is not possible for some workers to utilise the services. Khin Mar Hlaing, who is now second in command in one of the riverside factories in Mae Sot, explained:

> The employer said that only those who work in the factory are allowed to stay in the accommodation. But a nanny looking after the children does not work for the factory, right? So she is not allowed to stay. It is not fair... When the children are older they can go to a nursery. But there is only one nursery at the riverside [where the factories are]. So the children can go to the nursery while they are working. Most of the parents cannot take care of their kids while working so they send them back to their [home] village.

There is a growing use of paid childminders and childcare centres, especially in Mae Sot. Several nurseries now advertise in the factories. On the Burmese side of the border at Three Pagodas Pass there are currently three pre-school childcare centres, apparently charging similar rates, even though two are privately owned, the third being run by the local authority. Each centre cares for about twenty-five children aged 3 and upwards whilst their mothers are working in the factories on the Thai side of the border. It is also reported that there is a large temple on the Burmese side of the border which runs a primary school with boarding facilities; this caters mainly for the children of migrants working in Bangkok rather than in the border factories.

Away from the borders, it is harder to find Burmese childminders or nursery schools, and some workers have paid for Thai women to mind their children – though this is very expensive and women fear that their children will not be well cared for. May Thu Aye, a Mon worker, became pregnant after working in Samut Prakhan for five years. At the time of the interview she was not working because she was not happy to place her child in the care of a Thai childminder, so she and her husband decided to take their child back to Burma to be cared for by their relatives:

I cannot continue to work because my son is too young to be looked after by anyone else. I was not dismissed by the factory for delivery of the baby. I could place him with a Thai lady near my house by paying 60 baht a day, but I don't want to because she would not take good care of my son. She would be rough in handling my young baby so I need to look after him myself. By coming and working in Bangkok, I was not able to save money; instead I just had this baby.

Because workers have to work long hours, starting very early in the morning and often not finishing until nightfall, the option of keeping small children in Thailand, whether looked after by relatives or childminders, is also less than satisfactory. Many women also worry about remaining in Thailand away from their families and regret not being able to care of their now ageing parents.

Sabeh Han came to Bangkok six years ago and worked in garment factories. Before she married three years ago she was able to send money to her parents, but since she had her child she has only had irregular work and has barely been able to make ends meet, and even had to borrow from a money lender:

> I don't know when I can stay with together with my son. I would like to take care of him and my elderly mother. I left home when I was 26 years old... my sisters complain about me not being there to look after her, but there is nothing I can say because I can't always send enough money home to pay for my son's care, let alone my mother's. When I am able to send money I will tell them to take good care of him, but right now all I can do is ask them how my son is; I daren't say anything else... I feel I have failed.

Many migrant women expressed sadness that they were obliged to send their babies to be cared for by others, but the combination of economic need and the restrictive regulations in Thailand often give them no other option. Kaythi Min Soe has to rationalise her separation from her children by focusing on the hope that this is only temporary until she can earn enough to settle back home with them.

> Oh I cried every day when I first arrived. My husband's earning is just enough to buy food to eat. But now we are both working, I can use my wages to cover the children's expenses and any savings from my husband's earnings can be put towards building a house. That is why I need to be strong to work here, and one day definitely I will go back to my family to stay with my children. I always feel tired because I have to stand the whole day at work. Although I would like to quit the job, whenever I think about my children my tiredness fades away.

Many have mixed feelings: they miss their children, they worry about the burden on their families, and they are torn between wanting to move all their family to be near them in Thailand and wishing to maintain their roots and connections with their place of birth. Than Than Htun is 28 years old. There was a fire in her home town; she lost her house and had to move to a resettlement area. But the family was not able find work there, so three years ago she and her husband decided to come to Three Pagodas Pass, leaving their two daughters with her mother in Yangon.

> We plan to bring our daughters to live with us and to send them to school here. We feel sorry for our elderly parents having to look after our daughters. By having our daughters here with us, we will have more energy to work hard... I miss them. We can contact them by phone once a month. Whenever we call them, we cry. The oldest is now telling us to come back, but the youngest does not remember us since we left when she was only 1 year old... So I suffer for it. I just want to go back whenever I speak to them. Although we miss them we can't do anything about it because the job situation is so bad in Yangon that we cannot go back. If we go back, life will be even worse than it is now; so we comfort ourselves with the thought that this situation is only temporary.

But sometimes the separation proves too much and children are brought back from Burma to stay with their parents in Thailand. Hnin Wutyee Maw came to Mae Sot with her husband, her six-month-old baby and her mother, leaving her two older daughters behind with her sister. But she found it too difficult to be separated from the daughters and asked her mother to go back to Burma and bring the two girls to Mae Sot.

> It was only for four months that I was away from my two children. But I felt very bad and cried every day. I could not eat or sleep. I was missing them every day, and whatever I was doing I was worrying about them – whether they were eating well or in good health, what had happened to them that day, whether they were missing us and crying... I only felt better when I was able to bring them here, and now I have decided I can never stay far away from my children and family... Men never seem to cry because they are missing their children. But they also feel bad about being far away from the children. Women feel it more strongly because women are the ones who deliver the child from the womb and breastfeed them; men are the ones who earn money for food. That is the difference.

Health care

Although men take responsibility for economic support of the children, in the main it is women who have the emotional bond, and who take responsibility for the practical arrangements and the links with their families at home. And women also tend to take responsibility for accessing health services, not just for themselves but for other family members, often getting into debt in the process. Yee Kyaw came to Three Pagodas Pass five years ago with her parents and brothers and sister; she and her husband have responsibility for the well-being of the whole family.

> I borrowed money only one time in my life. I borrowed from my boss at the footwear factory to pay for my mother's medical care... She had paralysis twice in Burma. Last year the problem returned... She had to go to the clinic in Three Pagoda Pass, on the Burma side, spending something like 300 baht on every visit. To cover my mother's medical costs I borrowed 4000 baht with 20 per cent interest. And it took me a whole year working there to pay off the debt. I wanted to move to the mosquito net factory seven months ago, when they were hiring more workers, but I could not leave my present job until I had paid off the whole debt even though the wages are lower here.

Health services especially in the border areas are in theory, relatively generous to registered migrant workers, since they, like other low-paid workers in Thailand, can use the universal health-care scheme to access health care.[7] However, in Mae Sot most of the workers tended to use the Burmese-run Mae Tao clinic, which is also used by many residents on the Burmese side of the border, who say that it provides better and cheaper medical care than is available to them in their home towns. But the Burmese migrants also use the Mae Sot public hospital, particularly for acute and complex conditions. This has caused considerable resentment among local public officials, who have expressed concerns about the burden of migrant health care on Thai public services and finances.[8]

Some migrant workers told us that they had good reason to be grateful for the health services available to them in Thailand. One such is Su Su Win, who came to Mae Sot from Pegu when she was 16 years old to help ease her family's difficult economic situation. However, as she got married two years later against her parents' wishes she could not depend on family support when she had her daughter, so had to hire a local woman to care for the child when she returned to work. In her view the health care provided by the local hospital saved the child's life:

> My daughter is alive because we were in Mae Sot. With her condition, if we had been in Burma, my daughter would not have survived. Here [in Mae Sot] we can seek treatment in the hospital. In Burma there would be no way we could get treatment in the hospital free of charge.

Hsu Htet Htun got married and became pregnant after working in Three Pagodas Pass for two years. She told us how staff from a local NGO arranged for her to be treated in a Thai hospital after she suffered dangerous side effects as the result of an illegal abortion carried out in Burma:

> I went back home in April of this year because I was not in good health. Last year I got pregnant and had an abortion... but the bleeding did not stop for several months. A woman on the Burmese side of the border carried out the abortion – I only paid 300 baht as I was only one month pregnant. When I started bleeding, I went back to the clinic five or six times but the bleeding did not stop... Then with the help of the nurses from an NGO, I went to the health centre [on the Thai side] and they referred me to Sangkla hospital. The nurses helped me to get a border pass... I did not have [any] money but I received treatment in that hospital for nine days. Then they said I needed to have surgery, so they asked me to go back to Burma or go to Bangkok. But the nurse from the NGO said I should go to Kanchanaburi [the provincial centre] with a [referral] letter from Sangkla hospital. So I had the operation there, and stayed for nine days before coming back to Three Pagodas Pass. The hospital treatment costs 5,000 baht in Sangkla but I told them I only had 300 Baht, which they accepted. The charge for the treatment in the Kanchanaburi hospital amounted to 18,000 baht, but I didn't have any money so didn't have to pay.

Most migrant workers do not in fact use even the limited health services available. Several studies have demonstrated that Burmese migrant workers rarely attend public hospitals or health facilities; instead they tend to purchase medication directly from Burmese-speaking pharmacies, or attend NGO- or diaspora-funded clinics such as the Mae Tao clinic when they are available. In practice even registered migrant workers are rarely aware of their entitlement to public health services in Thailand, and their restricted mobility and lack of knowledge of the Thai language further limit the possibility of using such services.[9] They usually return to their homes in Burma if they or members of their family have any serious or chronic illnesses. Women's earnings are central to the family's ability to access health care in Burma. Khin Myint Aung, a factory worker in Mae Sot, told us that her husband's father had died the previous year after suffering from cancer for three years. They had sent back around 1 million kyats – the equivalent of their joint annual earnings – over the years to pay for his care, since he had no other source of funds. The general view was that treatment was cheaper but of inferior quality in Burma, but most people did not have the option of using medical services in Thailand. Even when they technically had an entitlement to health care, they were discouraged by their inability to speak Thai or by perceived or real hostility on the part of medical staff to Burmese migrants.

In the absence of other options the Burmese community in Mae Sot runs an insurance scheme to cover the funeral costs in the event of the death of migrant workers or their family members. The scheme has the support of churches and Buddhist temples, though it remains as an informal initiative since Thai regulations forbid 'aliens' from establishing independent organisations.

Education

The question of what happens to migrant children when they reach school age is clearly linked to issues of care and upbringing; but it also involves questions of citizenship and identity. Many workers in

Mae Sot send their children to one of the fifty-plus migrant schools in the town. Current estimates indicate that these schools serve some 10,000 children, though these are perhaps only a third of the Burmese children of school age living in the area.[10]

A range of overseas diasporic communities and international organisations from Europe, East Asia and North America[11] support the migrant schools and organisations promoting education in Mae Sot, such as the Children's Development Centre (CDC) and the BMWEC (Burmese Migrant Workers' Education Committee, a consortium of migrant schools). Some Burmese parents consider the quality of the migrant schools in Thailand to be better than the alternatives, and many schools recruit from non-migrant families in the bordering provinces. Parents hope that the trilingual system of education – Burmese, English and Thai – will be advantageous to their children's futures wherever that may be:

> I want to keep my children in the school here [in Mae Sot] until they have a level of education that can help them get jobs here. At least if they can write and speak good Thai and Burmese, they can get good jobs here [in Mae Sot]. (Chaw Su Lin)

However, the drawback is that these schools are not accredited by either the Burmese or the Thai education systems. Therefore, if the students go back to Burma their education in Mae Sot will not be recognised, and they will be unable to gain entrance to higher education establishments in their home country. There are also problems with progression to the Thai educational system. In spite of efforts being made to refer students to Thai schools, so that they will be able to go through the Thai educational system and achieve higher education, there are substantial obstacles both in terms of language and financially. Some larger learning centres, such as CDC, teach all the way up to grade 12, and support further education for its students. The Wide Horizon Program, supported by World Education, a US-based international NGO, provides students with practical community development skills so that they can go back to their communities and work for their societies.[12] However, the number of students that they can support is still limited, due to available NGO resources and to the support families can give to their children. At the same time, such migrant schools are only available in Mae Sot; in other places the only option is to attend a Thai school or go back to Burma for schooling.

Most workers in Three Pagodas Pass live on the Burmese side of the border and send their children to schools there. In any case, compared to Mae Sot, external funding is scarce and there are no diaspora schools serving the migrant community. There is one primary school that accepts migrant children in Sangklaburi district centre, but children of workers in Three Pagodas Pass are not able to get there because they would have to pass through an official immigration checkpoint en route, and, as we have explained, most of the workers lack official documentation. So they have no choice but to send their children to grade schools inside Burma – either in their home towns, or on the Burmese side of the Three Pagodas Pass border.

The general situation regarding migrant children's access to Thai schools is confusing. In theory, the Thai government, since 2005, has operated an 'Education for All' policy, which permits all children resident in the country to attend Thai public schools, regardless of their migrant or nationality status. This should mean that the children of migrant workers are eligible to go to school. Even though the registration scheme does not allow dependants to enter or remain in Thailand, once students are enrolled in Thai schools they are given a student ID that will allow them to go to attend. However, in reality, very few children of migrant workers are able to utilise this provision. First, there are no pre-school facilities for younger children. Second, the costs are substantial; even though tuition is free, parents routinely need to pay for uniforms and supplies, the cost of which is too high for migrants. Third, migrant children rarely speak Thai and there is no provision for non-Thai-speaking students in Thai public schools. And fourth, although the policy exists, few schools welcome migrant children with open arms and the majority still resist accepting them. Often schools refuse to take them on the grounds that they do not have space, or they require them to show household registration documentation, which can only be obtained if the family can find a Thai guarantor who agrees to the child being registered under his/her household. Such a requirement becomes a de facto rejection of the entry of migrant children.[13]

Moreover, the opinions of Thai officials and the public are often hostile to facilitating the education of migrant children in Thai schools. In this excerpt from a newspaper report,[14] a police officer expresses an attitude that is widespread in the country:

> Having migrant children studying in the town centre is also not appropriate, due to potential security problems. For safety, the migrant population should be in a restricted zone under state control. Also, if they want to study, their older peers should do the teaching, not our people... I cannot see how educating these children can benefit our country in any way. We have to think about the burden society must shoulder if these children decide to stay on.[15]

Migrant workers struggle to make decisions on whether they should keep their children with them or send them back to their families, and on what is the best education for the future of their children. This is difficult given the ongoing insecurities about their own futures in Thailand, and the hostile environment and precarious status that they have in both Thailand and Burma. Over half of the women to whom we talked expressed deep ambivalence about their future plans, particular with respect to their children's futures. As we have seen, many women, especially those with small children, viewed their sojourn in Thailand as a temporary measure to earn enough to support their families and to provide some kind of economic security for when they return home. But the situation still remains very volatile and uncertain within Burma, as the country moves towards the restoration of democracy, a process which has raised expectations regarding the possibility of political and economic change.

6

After the crisis:
new struggles and possibilities

The current global financial and economic crises have serious
implications for migrant workers worldwide. Past experience makes
us painfully aware that migrant workers, especially women workers
and those in irregular status, are among the hardest hit and most
vulnerable during crisis situations. While the full impact of the
crisis on migrant workers is yet to unfold, there are reports of direct
layoffs, worsening working conditions including wage cuts, increasing returns, and reductions in immigration intakes.[1]

Burmese migrant workers in the garment and knitting factories of
Thailand did indeed feel the brunt of the recent crisis as consumer
demand in Western countries fell sharply, resulting in retrenchment and shorter time working in the export factories where
they were employed. The Burmese women and men we spoke
to recounted their difficulties and dilemmas as they sought to
regain a toehold in the unstable labour market in Thailand, to
meet their obligations to their families at home, and to stabilise
themselves and their families in order to face the future. There was
a significant, if temporary, burgeoning of collective organisations
and negotiations among migrant workers in some locations. And
the Thai labour movement, traditionally indifferent if not hostile
to migrant workers, whom it has seen as weakening the bargaining

power and worsening the wage levels and working conditions of local labour, did mobilise to defend the rights of Burmese and other migrant workers within Thailand.

When the financial and economic crisis hit Thailand after the global credit crunch of 2008, the country was already embroiled in a political crisis, with a coalition government struggling to maintain stability and restore the confidence of external stakeholders. Tourism declined in the wake of the political conflicts, which led to the closure of Bangkok's international airport in 2008, and there was a reduction in investment and a collapse of Thailand's international credit rating. In 2009 there was a sharp downturn in the economy following over a decade of sustained economic growth, and a serious decline in exports, down 16.4 per cent in year-on-year comparisons with the first quarter of 2008. This amounted to a serious problem for the government, given that export earnings (including tourism) account for over 70 per cent of Thailand's GNP, which, on top of a drastic fall in (sales) tax revenues, further constrained the government's room for manoeuvre. At the same time there were serious ethnically driven uprisings in the South, where the population is majority Muslim,[2] and on the international relations front Thailand was losing influence to other regional powers such as China and Vietnam.

When the garment and textile industry began to experience reductions in export and domestic sales, resulting in layoffs and rising unemployment, the instinct of the government was to protect the local population at the expense of the migrant workforce. Unemployment in Thailand rose sharply from officially low levels in 2008/9, forcing the government to offer a range of unemployment benefits and social security payments to offset rising political discontent. In December 2008 the World Bank reported that a retrenched Thai factory worker was entitled to a 6,000 baht severance payment, and a monthly unemployment benefit of 3,000 baht, which represents more than a month's earnings with overtime for most migrant factory workers. However, such social security benefits were not extended to the thousands of Burmese migrant workers who were laid off in the factories of Mae Sot and Three Pagodas Pass. It would seem that the reluctance of Thai workers to take the 3D jobs occupied by migrant workers had not diminished in the face of the recession. The industrial labour market is in many ways a dual labour market, with quite different rates of pay, conditions and protection for Thai and migrant workers. When the downturn started to bite, most Burmese factory workers tried to adapt to the new conditions by accepting cuts in their wages and their working hours or piece rate pay, or by taking on less skilled jobs in agriculture or domestic sectors to tide them over until the hoped-for recovery took place.

In this chapter we outline the difficulties faced by the Burmese workers in our study as they tried to protect their livelihoods and their families from the effects of a global economic crisis, emanating from banking failures in the global North, which affected the purchase of export goods from countries like Thailand. As we explained in Chapter 1, migrant workers are at the insecure end of a long and complicated subcontracted supply chain – the least visible and the least protected. The response of the workers we spoke to was to be as flexible as possible in the circumstances, sacrificing their own well-being, their family arrangements, their regular financial remittances to their parents and siblings, and even their homes and security in order to keep alive the possibility of working in the export factories in future years when they hoped the situation would be better.

But the crisis also revealed the hostility of the environment in which these workers are located. Reports of increased harassment from both factory management and owners, from officials in the police, armed forces and government departments, and from the local Thai population, make more poignant the dilemma they are constantly confronted with – to stay or to return. But in spite of the obstacles, many workers are committed to sticking it out in Thailand, seeing a return to Burma as an unrealistic option in the foreseeable future due to ongoing commitments to their families and in the absence of any rapid or radical change in the political situation; so they calculate that they and their children are likely to have a better life if they stay in Thailand, however arduous and insecure their employment and living situation might be.

Effect of the economic crisis on migrant workers' employment in Thailand

The downturn in the ready-made garment and knitting industry came swiftly in the second half of 2008 and into 2009. *The Economist*[3] reported that, although total orders fell officially by only 12 per cent, the general decrease in demand had led to short-time working, cancellation of overtime, lay-offs and forced 'unpaid leave' in virtually all the factories in Mae Sot, as overall export demand dropped by over a quarter in that period. However, it is not possible to assemble unemployment figures in the conventional sense since a high proportion of the migrant workforce, especially outside of the Bangkok area, is unregistered. There were widespread reports that workers were dismissed at very short notice when orders dropped. Unskilled workers, who were in the main women, were more likely to lose their jobs, whereas factory owners tended to try to keep some kind of lien on their skilled workers in order to be able to respond competitively when the upturn in orders took place. Our survey revealed that nearly 60 per cent of migrant workers had found it difficult to find a job in 2008 compared to earlier years, and experienced longer periods of unemployment between jobs, particularly women, who were concentrated in the reserve labour pool of unskilled workers.

Migrant workers, especially women, are in many ways the shock absorbers of the economic crisis, not just in terms of the effect on their employment but also in terms of the ways in which they manage the challenges of the everyday and long-term survival of themselves and their families. Like others in Thailand, these workers were caught between falling incomes and rising prices. In a survey carried out by the MAP Foundation, which works with migrants all over Thailand, 85 per cent reported that they were in difficulties because rising prices made it impossible for them to make ends meet. All workers reported a fall in their earnings from factory work, with women more likely to report a loss of earnings.[4] The Bank of Thailand reported that inflation, in 2008, had reached an eleven-year high; whilst the official inflation rate was estimated to be between 7.5 and 8.8 per cent, the actual price hikes faced by workers were likely to be higher than this, since their accommodation, food and other costs are dependent on very closed markets where factory owners and traders are all scrambling to offset the effects of the localised recession. In the words of a woman working in Three Pagodas Pass, 'we are like a fish being fried in its own oil'.

Dealing with the crisis:
coping strategies of migrant workers

Migrant workers employ various strategies in face of the fall in real income and rising prices, and in response to the increased uncertainty arising from the effects of the crisis. Women in particular reported reducing their own and their families' food intake by having fewer meals a day, or by having smaller portions, or using inferior ingredients, although where possible they tried to protect the nutrition of their children. Many workers were forced to draw on their hard-earned savings in order to ensure that they could survive from day to day in the absence of any other form of assistance. Family and friends were also central to helping retrenched workers, and several reported that the diasporic organisations in Mae Sot, including the Buddhist temples, had provided food and other resources. And, as we have seen, some families who had been renting accommodation outside the factories told us that they had been forced to move to what are little more than shacks without water or electricity, in order to save money.

Other more long-term strategies were developed in order to try and secure the survival of the household. A small minority (2 per cent) in Mae Sot reported removing their children from school, and

4 per cent of the overall sample said they had been forced to send their children out to work. Child labour is extremely widespread among the Burmese migrant population, particularly in the border provinces in Thailand. But most migrant workers chose to keep their children in school, probably reflecting the fact that factory workers are relatively well educated in comparison with those who labour in the agricultural or construction sectors, and view their children's continuing schooling as an investment in the future. However, arrangements for the care of pre-school children were frequently changed in response to new circumstances. Nearly a quarter of all households questioned told us that they recently had to send one or more children back to their families in Burma, mainly on a temporary basis, it was hoped, in order to reduce the household's costs. A smaller number (4 per cent) had made the opposite arrangement – that is, sent for children currently living in Burma to join them in Thailand – possibly because they could not afford to maintain the regular remittances to cover their children's expenses in Burma, although, as we discuss below, migrant workers, especially women, did try to maintain their remittances for as long as possible.

Inevitably workers faced with a squeeze on their household budget frequently had to resort to borrowing money in order to survive; over 60 per cent of those in our study working in Mae Sot and Bangkok had resorted to credit. Although credit from different sources had always been important for migrants, who tend to live from hand to mouth, there had been a marked increase since the 2008 crisis. Family and friends were the chief source of informal finance, with men apparently having first call on the family finances. However, given that most people are in the same situation, many workers reported that it was difficult to get loans from friends, and even moneylenders were reluctant to advance funds, since the workers had little prospect of repaying in the near future.

Workers also reported that credit from employers during this time became important for their survival. This was not primarily because the factories were concerned with the welfare and survival of their workforce over this difficult period; rather, when they were obliged to cut back the hours or volume of employment because of falling orders, they frequently advanced the retrenched workers a small fraction of their previous wages. This meant that, rather than the workers leaving altogether in search of a more secure and regular income, the employer was able to ensure that there would be no problem recruiting or training new workers when demand picked up. Although the amount advanced was very little, equivalent to 500 baht a week, some of which was given in the form of rice and curry rather than money, workers were aware of the difficulties of finding other work in the circumstances, so accepted this minimal amount, for which they had to present themselves at the factory at an appointed time every day. One worker told us that this practice was akin to 'boiling a frog in a pot. If they put the frog in the water and slowly raise the temperature, the frog does not notice that it is getting hotter and hotter, so does not jump out – and ultimately dies.' The implication was that the workers would starve slowly and not resist or take any action that would threaten the plans of the factory to maintain its market position. However, as we demonstrate below, a few workers were provoked into taking collective action in the face of the declining situation within the factories.

The crisis and the squeeze on household finances also put pressure on the level of remittances that workers were able to send back to Burma. Some 36 per cent of women respondents and 47 per cent of male respondents said that they had been forced to reduce the amount of money they sent home to their families. MAP Foundation reported that there was a significant drop in the amount workers were able to send back home, because of the extra hardships caused by the recession.

> I could not remit money since I lost my job four months after the economic crisis. My husband has a regular job, but the payments are very erratic and he has not received any wages for the last three months and the owner only gives him 500 baht a week as a loan. So,

we don't have enough money to remit. We even had to sell gold to
pay for food and accommodation, and had to seek a 1,000 baht loan
from the employer to pay the rent, (Sandar Aye, Mae Sot)

The ability of workers to send money back to their families
was affected not just by the reduction in income and the rise in
the cost of living in Thailand but also because the appreciation of
the Burmese currency (the kyat) caused by the inflow of foreign
funds after the Nargis cyclone in early 2008 had reduced the local
value of remittances from migrant workers. However, as reported
in Chapter 3, women workers tended to maintain a minimal level
of financial support to their families even when their earnings
declined. This is a further illustration of how Burmese women have
had to absorb the negative effects of the crisis, often prioritising
the welfare of their families at the expense of their own health and
well-being. This is to be explained partly in terms of the gendered
nature of filial duty in Burma, where women have traditionally
felt obligations to their families throughout their lives, whereas
men have transferred their primary responsibilities in their adult
lives to their new families. But also, as we saw in Chapter 5,
women are mindful of the life course support they depend on from
their families, particularly when they have children of their own,
and their remittance behaviour can also be seen as a strategy to
maintain the mutual obligation between themselves and relatives
back home.

Retrenchment and strikes

Even before the economic crisis, migrant workers in Mae Sot had
organised strikes and other actions in defence of their rights at
work, and to protest against gross violations, which reportedly
included physical and sexual abuse – and even murder – of workers
by factory owners, management and police, non-payment of wages,
and an intolerable deterioration in working conditions.

Because of the large numbers of Burmese workers in Mae Sot
and the fact that their numbers have been growing steadily since

the mid-1990s, there are a large number of organisations located in the town which have supported workers in their struggles, in spite of the legal ban on migrant workers establishing their own organisations. MAP foundation, which is based in Chiang Mai, has an office in Mae Sot, and has been active in supporting workers who seek to take their cases to court when their employers or others have clearly transgressed what little protection they do enjoy under the law, such as non-payment, or arbitrary detention or abuse. MAP is also one of the co-founders of the Yaung Chi Oo Workers' Association (YCOWA), which is specifically dedicated to achieving fair wages and working conditions for migrant workers, documenting abuse, and carrying out training and legal education. Another organisation active in supporting migrant workers' rights and offering legal aid in the case of disputes with employers is the Burma Labour Solidarity Organisation (BLSO), which is supported by the Australian Confederation of Trade Unions (ACTU). There is also the Labour Law Clinic, which was established in late 2005 by the Human Rights and Development Foundation and is funded entirely by the US international union network, the AFL–CIO. The Federation of Trade Unions – Burma (FTUB), an underground trade union in Burma supported by the ITUC and recognized by the ILO, also operates in Mae Sot, though it has no legal status there. The Thai Labour Campaign, an NGO campaigning for the rights of precarious workers in Thailand, has more recently extended its remit to support migrant workers and has conducted a number of workshops and training courses in Mae Sot in conjunction with local organisations. There are also a number of welfare-based NGOs and diasporic organisations in Mae Sot, including Social Action for Women (SAW), the Mae Tao Clinic (discussed in Chapter 5), and others supporting orphaned children, education and health projects. The Committee for the Promotion and Protection of Child Rights on the Thai–Burma border (CPPCR) supports migrant parents with newborn babies, helping them acquire birth certificates so that their children will not be stateless. In addition, the international NGO World Vision has a programme in Mae Sot linked specifically to HIV prevention and education among the migrant population.

This contrasts with the situation in Three Pagodas Pass, where the only organisation operating to support migrant workers is the Pattanarak Foundation, which works with other organisations such as the Action Network for Migrants, the Border Essan Action Network (BEAN) and several (Protestant) church organisations to deliver welfare assistance to migrants. No organisation in this area focuses specifically on the labour rights of migrant workers.

Since the crisis, legal action, strikes, occupations and other collective protests have been more frequent in Mae Sot. Between 2002 and 2009, the Yaung Chi Oo Workers Organization has supported 148 labour disputes. The disputes involved a range of issues, including non-payment of wages over two or three months, low wages and piece rates, non-payment of overtime rates, demands for the legal minimum wage (which at the time was 151 baht per day with 27 baht per hour overtime), and unfair dismissal. There are also numerous small-scale disputes that do not end up in court; in some factories these occur two or three times a year.

Between December 2008 and February 2009, eight factories, including some large plants, were closed down in Mae Sot, and the level of worker protests and strikes escalated. The following accounts of strikes in four garment factories in Mae Sot give an indication of worker militancy following the economic crisis of 2008.

Factory A is a fairly large knitting factory owned by a Hong Kong Chinese company. It previously employed 1,000 workers but this declined to 650 as many workers left their jobs because the working conditions were too demanding. The dispute started in October 2008 over a complaint by the workers that the hours were excessive and they were forced to work overtime. They frequently worked a fifteen-hour day, often working until midnight or even later. But they were not paid for the extra hours, because they were on piece rates. They were not permitted any day off in the week, nor allowed to take annual leave. Due to the rising cost of living, the workforce decided they could no longer tolerate this situation so they formed a committee of ten workers (six men, four women) from the 650-strong workforce. Initially, all the workers joined the protest. Their immediate demand was modest: although the legal overtime rate was a supplement of 28 baht an hour, the workers requested a supplementary payment of only 5 baht an hour in addition to their basic wage. The factory owner, knowing the difficulties the workers would have in finding alternative employment, decided to play hardball and offered only 3 baht an hour overtime. The response from the workers was divided between those who were prepared to accept the offer, and others who wanted to hold out for the full 5 baht. Some 45 per cent of the total workforce voted to continue the struggle, with nearly 57 per cent of the women workers refusing to accept the employer's offer. The factory owner tried to enlist the support of the police, demanding that they arrest the workers' representatives, but the police were forced to withdraw when the massed ranks of protesting workers surrounded their cars. The workers brought the case to the Labour Protection Office, which extracted a verbal promise from the employer that they would be paid a daily wage of 151 baht a day from January 2009. Tin Nwe Soe, a worker from Yangon in her early twenties, had studied economics at college for two years. She came to Mae Sot five years ago to join her sisters, who were working in the factory. With the support of her mother and siblings she decided to take on the responsibility of being the workers' representative:

> I was very busy during the time we were negotiating an increase in the daily wage rate. While the other workers were working in the factories I had to go to the Labour Protection Office, and whenever the manager asked we had to stop working and go to solve whatever problem had arisen (including problems regarding discipline and productivity)... Every day after we finished work, I had to go and visit the other workers, room by room, to talk about the rights of workers... I also had to go to the Labour Protection Office when they called me. Whenever I came back from the Labour Protection Office, the workers wanted to know what had been discussed, so I had to go once again room by room to explain.

Not only were the workers not permitted to form their own union; they did not even have a place where they could get together to talk, which was why the leaders had to visit them one at a time.

In January 2009, the employer was still refusing to agree to the daily wage rate determined by the Labour Protection Office, and insisted that if the workers wanted to be paid a daily wage they would have to leave the factory accommodation, which he said he was subsidising. In a remarkable example of organisation the leaders found rooms outside the compound for all the protesting 294 workers, and they moved out of the factory dormitories. After a further twenty-four days the employer suddenly announced that all the workers living outside the factory would be dismissed. The workers then decided to submit the case to court to demand compensation for their sudden dismissal. The Labour Protection Office, however, ruled that it could only accept a maximum of twenty cases a day, which meant that there was a prolonged process, lasting several months, of preparing all the documentation for the workers, which involved the members of the workers' committee accompanying each group of workers to the Labour Protection Office every day. Tin Nwe Soe continued:

> Since that time, nineteen girls who did not want to face the problems of going to court or to the government offices decided to return to Burma. The problem is that these young Burmese girls are afraid of official offices and courts in Thailand. Every single worker was obliged to go to the Labour Protection Office to fill in the forms to request compensation, and these young women wanted to avoid doing that so they went back to Burma.

There was also pressure from home for women to return. Many parents called their daughters to ask them to return to Burma, because they were afraid of what might happen in Mae Sot, although they were fully aware that if the workers returned they would forfeit their right to compensation. Some of the workers as well as the parents were worried that if they were involved in protests in the factories, they would be labelled as political activists, and linked to anti-government movements in Burma, so would have problems if they returned to the country. The protest has divided families. One of Tin Nwe Soe's sisters went back to Burma after submitting her compensation claim; she was accompanied by her husband, who in common with his parents – also employed at that factory – had not participated in the protest. This had caused tension within the family, so the sister decided that the whole family should return to Burma in order to avoid the difficult situation with his parents.

We noted that both women and men carried out the full range of tasks required of the workers' representatives, including visiting the Labour Protection Office, talking to the workers and helping them fill in the required documentation to file their claims. Nevertheless, men were represented disproportionately on the committee. The leaders' explanation for this was that women had to carry a heavier burden of family support, so they could not afford to join the protest for an extended and indefinite period, and risk being without any income at all. In the end, only three of the original ten leaders (two men and one woman – our respondent Tin Nwe Soe) remained as active leaders. Although the leaders shared the work related to organising the protest equally, there was still a gender division of labour in domestic work:

> The ten workers' representatives moved into the office of Burma Labour Solidarity Organization to stay there, as we had no income and therefore could not rent any rooms for ourselves. But in the mornings, I would get up at 6 o'clock and cook food for all of us – I had to do the cooking because the other leaders were men, who didn't know how to cook, although they did help me.

The absence of any wages was a difficult issue for the workers' representatives. Of the three leaders who remained involved in the protest in Factory A, none of them had immediate family commitments. One of the men was married but he did not feel obliged to support his family in Burma; the other man was single. Both men were supported by friends in Mae Sot. The female leader, Tin Nwe Soe, was also single and had the support of her sisters and other family members who worked in Mae Sot. Although there was no formal arrangement, the workers each gave a donation of 20 baht to support the leaders when they visited the office.

The consequences of taking a leadership role in this struggle were serious and long-lasting:

> [After the protest in Factory A], I had no choice but to get another job as I needed to earn some money. I started to work in the Mae Pa knitting factory in June [2009] but unfortunately, three days after I started working there a dispute began between the workers and the owner regarding piece rates. I did not want to get involved in this case because I still had to resolve my own situation. However, whilst the workers were discussing how to move forward, the Palm Gang[5] entered the factory searching for a worker whose photo they had. I was surprised to be informed by one of the other women workers that the photo was of me, so I left the factory quietly before they could find me. I realized that a notorious (Thai) street gang, who are given a free hand in Mae Sot to do whatever they like, wanted me for something. I thought it better to quit the job. Then I got a job in this factory, which is owned by a local policeman, but I had to change my name first. (Tin Nwe Soe in Mae Sot)

There was another dispute in a large ready-made garment factory owned by a Chinese-Thai businessman. The dispute in Factory B started two months later in August 2008. The factory employed a total of 350 workers, of whom 200 were women. The dispute arose because the workers complained that about a third of the workforce was being given preferential treatment in terms of workload and wages. The complaint turned to anger when, in August 2008, the piece rate was lowered from 70 baht to 60 baht per dozen. So those workers who felt discriminated against launched a complaint and requested that they be paid a daily wage. This was agreed on condition that they moved out of the factory compound and found new accommodation. Pwint Phyu, who became one of the protest leaders, told us it was very difficult to find accommodation for 220 workers:

It was not easy to search for rooms for such a large number of workers in a short space of time. In addition, most of the workers had never really been outside the factory compound. They had worked every day from morning until night inside the factory, without knowing anything about the surrounding area in Mae Sot.

The protesting workers began to be paid at a daily rate. However, the employer began to harass them, attempting to stop them entering the factory, or deliberately provoking them by paying higher allowances to non-protesting workers. In the end, the protesting workers were told that the factory had closed down, even though other workers were still working inside. So the protesters filed a complaint and a demand for compensation with the Labour Protection Office.

Pwint Phyu Maw explained that her decision to become a leader was practical rather than born of any political ambition:

> I didn't particularly want or intend to become a leader. The male leaders told us that they needed at least two women to join them in order to appeal to the sympathy of the officials at the Labour Protection Office so that we could talk about the suffering of the workers, which would increase the chances of getting the demands heard. No one else volunteered, so two of us decided to do it. Usually women do not want to become leaders as they have little knowledge of the law or workers' rights, and are too timid to speak to the officials in the Labour Protection Office. Worst of all, they are afraid that the boss will ask someone to kill the leaders, so their parents forbid them to become leaders. However, my parents encouraged me; they said I should do what I felt was right. If I wanted to come back to Burma, then I could; if I wanted to stay in Mae Sot that was OK with them as well. But it was the men who were in charge, and when they needed me to go with them to the Labour Protection Office they would call me.

However, once she had accepted the responsibility she was determined to pursue the struggle:

> We can never forget about the events that we have encountered during our working days in the factory. Before the crisis, we just asked the owner to respect our rights to get higher piece rates. At

the time, we were OK with him. But how he dealt with the problems that arose after the crisis and the way he took his revenge against us because of our legitimate demand made us feel deeply hurt... I will never again enter any of the factories here in the future. All the factories here exploit the workers in some way or another.

Sandar Aye's experience in Factory C illustrates the insecurity that has been increasing since the 2008 crisis. She had been working for three years in a medium-sized garment factory with 200 workers in Mae Sot owned by a Thai businessman, but then there was a protest and all the workers lost their jobs. The factory was very strict. They employed only women workers, on the grounds that they were obedient, docile and would not create problems. The management did not allow the workers to leave the factory compound or to receive guests, except on one Sunday a month. The protest occurred in response to the harsh treatment meted out to the Burmese workers by the Thai women guards charged with policing them. After a year and a half the workers did receive compensation. Sandar Aye moved to a different factory, but after three months there was another protest there and she lost her job again. The case went to court but there was no committee or leadership to support the workers and in the end nothing happened.

Many workers are well aware of the obstacles and difficulties faced by migrant workers if they want to pursue their legal rights. According to Khin Mar Hlaing, who works as a supervisor in a garment factory in Mae Sot:

When a labour issue is brought before the court there is a lengthy official procedure. In the meantime, the employer often tries to persuade the workers to resume their work, promising that the wages will be increased by this or that amount. Since the workers cannot afford to be jobless for a long time, many workers on strike choose to go back to work in the same factory, on the basis of such an agreement, so those who are leading the protest are left without any followers. From the workers' perspective, they would calculate that if they transferred to a new factory, they would have to sort out a range of issues, including their present ID cards,[6] any extension of their ID cards, as well as fees for transferring to a new employer, and

they have no guarantee that the new employers will support their
application to renew their ID cards. There are so many issues... The
workers also think that they have come to Mae Sot to earn money
– not to end up with problems. If they get involved in the workers'
strike, they will not be paid their daily wage until their court case
has been completed. For them, it is not possible to return to their
villages without any money... So the majority do not want to have
problems because they know that they will lose out in the end.

There was a dispute in another fairly large knitting factory,
owned by a Taiwanese businessman, who is based in Bangkok.
Factory D is a long-established concern with 700 workers, many
of whom have been working there for over ten years. The dispute
started because of non-payment of wages for two or three months
in March 2009. The factory announced that it was under threat
of closure due to lack of orders, and the workers were put on
reduced time of between three and ten days' work a month. The
management had rented a building outside the factory compound
for the accommodation of workers, but because of the lack of
business it was no longer able to pay the rent, so the workers were
forced to move into the factory compound. Since the factory was
not paying their wages, it supplied them with a limited amount
of food – vegetable curry and rice twice a day; however, this was
not enough for them to survive on, so they had to cook additional
food themselves. The workers built a makeshift communal kitchen
in the factory compound to prepare the food. They also collected
money from the workforce and were further supported by donations
from those still employed in Mae Sot, as well as from Bangkok, and
indeed from other businesses who were sympathetic to the workers.
The workers had to cut wood from trees and shrubs to take into
the factory compound to use as fuel. They also established a social
welfare association among themselves. Many of the workers were
skilled, with long service at this factory, so were reluctant to move
to other workplaces where they would have to begin again as new
workers, at a lower pay rate, and feared they would not be able to
obtain registration documents if they changed employers. Some

workers, mainly women, thought it was not worth remaining in Mae Sot with little hope of compensation, so returned to Burma. Many of the others were forced to move to one of the riverside factories, where the pay is much lower and there is no chance of registration, but they were anxious to obtain some kind of income.

Thein Kyaw is one of the women leaders. She is a single Burman woman in her early thirties who completed her education to grade 8 in Burma. She has been working in Mae Sot for ten years and is an experienced machinist. She recalled:

> When I returned from Burma in March [2009], I found out that there was this problem of non-payment in our factory, and the workers had initiated a complaint to the Labour Protection Office... I became a leader in April. The officer from the Labour Protection Office tried to avoid meeting us. Every time we went there, his staff said he was not there even though he was in the office. Then he promised that our wages would be paid on May 20th at 2 p.m. and they would also give us rice and curry for the time we were not paid between 7 and 20 May. They did in fact give us curries, but they had no oil or meat, only vegetables – we could not eat them like that. But we needed food so we did not complain about the quality because we planned to make a complaint about this as well when we met the employer at the court in the presence of the lawyer and the officials from the Labour Office. We had kept a record of all our grievances – that they don't provide sufficient clean water for us, which is why last week the workers got diarrhoea and the staff from the hospital had to come to our factory and treat all the workers who were suffering. Now we have to buy purified water to drink.

In the end, in May 2009, the workers received 50 per cent of their two months' unpaid salary, but were ordered to vacate the factory. Workers were happy to receive at least some payment, but most people had run up debts whilst they had not been paid. On the day they were paid many of their creditors came to the factory demanding repayment of debts, which had by then multiplied because of the 20 per cent monthly interest rate charged. The creditors were fighting among themselves about whose debts should be settled first. The workers were also nervous about their registration, which had to be renewed with the employer, and they were not confident that this factory would renew it. If they wanted a three-month renewal of registration with a new employer, they would need to pay 1,650 baht, compared to the 550 baht extension fee with their existing employer, the fee for changing their employer being 550 baht, with a further 550 baht payable to register with the new employer.

The stress and desperation that this caused the workers is reflected in the testimony of Ye Ye Khaing:

> Oh I don't want to get mixed up with Thai people by going to court and to the offices. We will never win and get our rights by going to the offices and court... The compensation is unthinkable for us. You know we also have rights to get compensation after working here for ten years because the factory closed down. According to the laws we should get the compensation. But I don't want to go to the court to ask for it. We will never win the case because we do not have rights like the Thais.

Ye Ye Khaing is a 40-year old woman from Mon state. Initially, she was not keen to travel to Thailand, but she came to Mae Sot because her father asked her to accompany her two younger sisters. She was married and had children at that time. Since she was earning good wages she stayed on with the aspiration of buying farmland in Burma, but now with the trouble in the factory she feels she needs to stick it out to get the compensation. One of the male leaders who were present during our interview with Ye Ye Khaing described the situation using a Burmese saying, *sout le su, sar le yu, nanle mu* ('If we go back we will injure ourselves with a sharp thing; if we eat the food, it will make us a fool; if we touch it, it will make us dizzy').

Despite the number of organisations supporting workers in obtaining their legal rights, the risks to the workers, as well as the immediate costs in terms of wages forgone, accommodation lost and problems with their registration and identity cards, are generally too high for most to get involved in strikes and protests.

Harassment, xenophobia and prejudice

The lives of migrant workers are made difficult not only by exploita-tive working conditions and their precarious status but also by the hostility and harassment they experience in Thailand. Thai newspapers repeatedly advance the notion that all migrants are a security threat, use public resources and steal jobs that rightfully belong to Thais, and claim that the children of Burmese migrant workers will overrun Thailand. This public discourse has become more widespread since the 2008 crisis, and has been reinforced with every successive political crisis in Thailand. The *Daily News* on 1 January 2011 carried one such report

> The Prime Minister expressed his concern about the impact that migrant workers might have on national security. Hence, he com-manded relevant agencies to review policy.
>   Prime Minister Abhisit Vejjajiva gave an interview about security issues saying that he anticipated more problems in the future. Therefore the government would continue to enforce the law in order to bring about peace and end the conflict in the three Southern provinces. To this end, Article 21 of the Internal Security Act would be implemented in March this year [2011] in accordance with initiatives of projects for administration of Southern provinces. Another concern was the problems of migrant labour that affected national security. He requested the Ministry of Labour to review its policy about the management of migrant labour in the light of the fact that most migrant workers did not register for a work permit, whilst many of those who had obtained work permits faced problems of nationality verification.

Before national holidays there are frequent reports of raids on migrant communities intended to 'prevent crimes'.[7] Reports of arrests of migrant workers are routinely accompanied by observa-tions that crimes by migrants are on the increase, although this picture is not necessarily accurate.[8] A review of reports in the largest circulation Thai language newspaper, *Thai Rat*, between January 2010 and March 2011 demonstrated that, although half of the crimes reported were committed by migrant workers, there were an equal number of cases in which migrant workers were the victims of crimes.[9]

There are also frequent sensationalist reports about the threat of overpopulation caused by uncontrolled 'breeding' by migrant workers. Fearing that migrant workers' children would overrun the country, the minister of labour, Chalermchai Srion, proposed that migrant workers should be pressured into using birth control. He believed that this was the right solution and employers would be informed about the plan regardless of criticism.

> Concerning migrant workers' children, we have no idea how many of them are born in Thailand each year. But there are many of them and we have no precise policy to deal with it. We are now thinking about the solution. Some countries impose restrictive policies of sending pregnant migrant workers back home. Therefore, migrant workers must use birth control. If not, they must be sent home. According to humanitarian principles, we have to provide support for their children. But it's better to prevent the problem. Personally, I think that migrant workers should have birth control. We have to inform them about it and realise that they come here to work. (*Krungthep Thurakit*, November 2010)

Newspapers also carry open letters by the general public to members of parliament, complaining about migrant children attending school while some Thai children are not able to. One such letter claimed that

> Crimes such as drugs and robbery are a consequence of the influx of migrants. Meanwhile, it is difficult to solve the problem because state officers hesitate to deal with NGOs and UNHCR. Besides, state officials have an obligation under the national basic education policy that aimed to provide equal education to all children in Thailand... I accept that the Office of Provincial Education has not yet done anything about these centres because there is no law directly controlling the learning centres for migrant children. Hence, the number of these learning centres rapidly increases. Meanwhile, we found that almost every learning centre uses the Burmese curriculum to teach. No Thai teachers are found in these schools and Thai language is not taught. There are concerns about the hidden agenda of these actions.[10]

Such views reflect ill-informed resentment about the ways in which the migrant community has to organise its own facilities such as schools for migrant children since they are not catered for within the Thai public system. These views stir up conflict between Thais and Burmese migrants. The article below from an English-language newspaper reflects popular fears that the local population is being swamped by migrants, but also that the authorities and the government do not defend the interests of Thai citizens:

> A few days ago I went to a Burmese migrant workers' community in Samut Sakorn. Burmese have settled everywhere either in the prawn market or nearby... All the shops selling consumer goods, CDs, and barber shops and [illegal] clinics for Burmese made me feel like I was walking in Naypyidaw [the new capital of Burma].
>
> If you walk to this community alone, you would be watched with hostile eyes as if you were a stranger invading their community. There are voices behind you with language you don't understand. How could this happen? This is Thailand, isn't it? This community had everything like in Burma. My young friend who was working at the hospital there told me that many Burmese women were brought to the hospital with strange symptoms. The doctor's diagnosis reported finding sharp, long bamboo sticks inside their wombs, which he assumed was caused by illicit abortion...
>
> However, I would like to address the problem about Burmese migrant workers to the authorities and related agencies. If they want to just ignore this problem, they should resign or move to work in another province. Then there will be places for good officers to save Samut Sakorn from being occupied by the Burmese. Quick action must be undertaken at least for the sake of our King Naresuan.[11]

Such prejudice and xenophobia are resented by the migrant workers, who complain that Thai people rarely appreciate the contributions they make to the Thai economy, or the reasons they feel compelled to leave their homes and families in Burma to work in such exploitative and hostile conditions. Aung Naung, a Tavoy man, now employed in a garment factory in Mae Sot but with several years experience of working in Samut Prakan, said:

As you know, Thais don't want to do the jobs that Burmese are doing nowadays. Who will do these jobs if the Burmese are not in Thailand? We also want to go back and stay in our own country where we don't have to be afraid of the police and people like the Palm Gang who attack Burmese people on the road at night. But the price of goods is very high in Burma and it is very difficult to find work... Nobody wants to stay in someone else's country but we have no choice... Some Thai people don't have a good impression of the Burmese. One day when I went to a Thai house to do some construction work, the owner did not allow any of the Burmese workers to enter his house... the owner thought all Burmese are thieves because the house had been burgled a few weeks earlier. Some Thai people hate the Burmese. I don't know why. [Maybe] because our old ancestors attacked their country... One day when we were in our room a Thai man passed by. A Burmese man was talking and laughing with his friend but the Thai guy thought that the Burmese were laughing at him so he attacked him and nobody dared to defend him. Because this is not our country and we don't have ID we can't defend ourselves. If we do, we will be sent back.

May Hnin Khaing, a Karen woman in her forties who came to Bangkok when she was 22 years old to work in a fish canning factory near Bangkok, reflected on the suffering of migrant workers:

My friend asked me if I wanted to be an agent, bringing people from the villages to Bangkok, but you know it is very dangerous. We saw on the TV how people being smuggled in a refrigeration truck had died. If I was carrying a child and something happened I would also be in trouble and everybody would be sad – not only the children's parents but also me. The life of the Burmese people is very sorrowful, tough, bad and pitiful. You see, here [in Thailand] it is better, [but] go and look at the other side of the building – the rooms are like pigeon holes, no water – just a small tank for all the people in the building. Dirty, small rooms – Oh we Burmese are suffering a lot of trouble here. If our government was good we would not have to suffer like this. We are also oppressed by the Thais... Of course, if all the Burmese go back home this tin fish factory will only have ghosts. No Thais want to work here.

It is clear that the crisis has increased the hostility of the Thai government and population to the presence of migrant workers, as well as worsening their working and living conditions, and increasing their vulnerability and insecurity. But in spite of this many workers insist on trying to remain and build a life in Thailand rather than return to the privations and oppression they face in Burma.

After the crisis – to stay or to return?

According to our interviews around 90 per cent of the workers still wanted to return for visits to their home villages or towns, particularly for special occasions such as the New Year festivals, which take place in April, although some 60 per cent were determined to remain working in Thailand in the short and medium term.

As we discussed in Chapter 5, many women return in order to deliver their baby in Burma or take it back to be taken care of by their parents. Others go back for health reasons, because they are too sick to work or unable or unwilling to access medical care in Thailand. Migrants also told us that they tend to return home after they have experienced a period of extreme hardship in Thailand such as delayed or non-payment of wages, or having to pay fines or bribes to the immigration authorities or the police, or when they have been cheated out of money by employers, agents or traders. However, we found very few cases where they voluntarily returned to their place of origin once they had earned enough money and wanted to settle down, though many expressed this as a goal for the future.

Although Burmese migrant workers do look forward to the time they can go back to Burma, they think this will not be possible until they are too old or too sick to work, as their priority is to continue to earn money in Thailand. Meanwhile they are resigned to the hostility of the Thai people, as Kyaw Lin, a man of 70 resident in Thailand since 2004, whose four daughters are working in Mae Sot, explained:

> Thais are not good to the Burmese; they just think the Burmese are slaves; they don't think the Burmese are human beings. They are

rude to those who come and work in their country... For us every-
thing is difficult – to travel, to stay, to work, to practice religion,
health, even to die – in all aspects. That is why we are now thinking
seriously [about going back] since our health becomes weaker and
weaker.

Plans to return are often projected into the distant future. Htet
Htet Hlaing is in her late thirties; she has worked for the past ten
years, together with her husband; two of their children live with
them. She has just sent her ten-month-old daughter back to Burma
for her mother to look after. Although committed to remaining in
Thailand while she can work and earn money, she looks forward
to the day when all of them will be able to return home:

> We cannot tell exactly when we will go back forever, because many
> of the people who returned to their home towns had to come back
> to Bangkok again because Thailand has a big spirit. One thing for
> sure is that I will not stay here forever because I would like to live in
> my home town again, when I am old. Last time I visited my family
> in Burma, I did not want to stay there for long because we had only
> expenses and no income. We spend a lot of money when we visit our
> relatives. After three days, I just wanted to come back [to Thailand]
> to earn money... But when we get old, Burma is a suitable place for
> us to live. We can go to the monasteries to practise our own religion.
> We can stay in our own community. I want to be together with my
> mother and siblings again. Here [the place where she is staying in
> Bangkok] we help each other by staying together. Here the [Bur-
> mese] community is very good.

The crisis raised the issue of return for many workers who
were finding it difficult to continue to work and make a living in
Thailand. However, many of those who did return home soon came
back to seek work in Thailand, since their families continued to
depend on their earnings.

> Many workers decided to go back to Burma when their earnings
> dropped maybe to less than 600 baht a month – which is just enough
> to buy food but not to save. Then they started to worry about their
> children and family members they have left in Burma. 'Oh, how are
> my kids going to survive, since I cannot send money?', 'My parents

might be in debt by now because I cannot send money', 'How can
I repay such debts?' – many thoughts are in their minds and they
returned to their villages. But in their villages, they cannot earn any
money and encounter difficulties in surviving. So then they come
back [to Thailand] again to look for a job. So in the lean season most
of the workers have difficulties. (Khin Mar Hlaing of Mae Sot)

Khin Mar Hlaing has herself been in Thailand since 1998. Her
grandparents had worked in Thailand since 1988, and she can
speak Thai well. But she still thinks about returning some time
in the future to her sister's house in Burma.

Migrants are clear about the conditions that need to be met if
they are to return home on a permanent basis. Most important
is the presence of surviving parents and family at home and also
ownership or shares in assets such as land and a house. But without
prospects of employment many are reluctant to return, and there
are widespread stories about the Burmese government's practice
of imposing arbitrary taxes on any property owned by individuals
(from motorbikes to televisions), the forced planting of crops that
are not necessarily appropriate to the particular location, the
confiscation of agricultural land, forced conscription and forced
labour, which make migrants fearful of their prospects if they
return.

One of the migrants we interviewed in June 2008 in Three
Pagodas Pass told us that it was no longer possible to survive
in the villages in Mon and Karen states. In 2009-10 there were
armed militias from both government and opposition groups,
including the government- backed Democratic Karen Buddhist
Army (DKBA) and the KNU (Karen National Union), as well as the
military government itself, all demanding taxes (*set kyay*) every
month. The villagers refer to these groups as 'beggars', since they
demand money from the villagers for their survival. Forced labour
(*loke ah pay*) for the SPDC military is still compulsory; each
household has to send one of its members to carry out such work,
or is liable to a fine of 7,000-8,000 kyats per month (equivalent
to around 200 baht – some 20 per cent of what garment factory

workers could earn in Yangon in a month, which is itself too low for a family to survive on), which means that most families depend on the remittances from migrant workers in Thailand to survive.

Families frequently operate a collective strategy, with some siblings returning to look after elderly parents, leaving others in Thailand to work. The dream is to accumulate enough capital in order to invest in a potential income-generating business in Burma. Ye Ye Soe came to Thailand with her husband in 1995; four children later, she and her husband are still working in Mae Sot:

> I will not go back to my home town in this situation without having saved some money. I have to stay and work here for many years to have capital to invest back in Burma. If the situation was favourable I'd like to stay here [in Mae Sot]. But I don't want to stay here for good because my father and all my other relatives are back in Burma. As Burma is my own country, my real community is only there. But I definitely won't be able to go back there at the moment – even for the next few years. When I have enough, I'd like to stay in my home town by establishing my own sewing shop in my house.

At least half of the workers we interviewed in Bangkok and Mae Sot were considering going back to Burma after the crisis, blaming the deteriorating safety and environment in these areas. But others have to face the reality that there is no easy road back. If they have sold land or houses in order to raise the money to come to Thailand, they may have no place to return to. Families have very often been totally reorganised around migrant members. This was the case for Ma Maw Cho in Samut Prakhan; four of her eight siblings now work in Thailand, while the parents and other siblings are at Three Pagodas Pass on the Burmese side. They fled their home village when she was 10 years old because of the fighting between KNU and SPDC. Her brother was blinded by a mine, and he is now in Yangon in a home for the blind. Thus her family are all scattered and there is no place she can call her home. Ma Maw Cho and her siblings send money to support their elderly mother, who has relocated to live near the border; so the adult children no longer have a home in their village of origin.

Kyaw Lin, the father of May Thin Aye, said that families can become estranged and workers frequently lose their links home:

> The parents of our neighbours came to live with them in Mae Sot, but when we were all arrested and deported their parents were frightened and returned to Burma and have not even visited again. The people who have lost their houses and families in Burma cannot go back home – they have no prospects for a better life in Burma.

But, ironically, having a family network back in Burma can also serve as an obstacle to return, especially when the workers lose control of the use to which remittances are put. Hnin Wutyee Maw was working in a house factory in Mae Sot, but got frightened by a number of murders and rapes that took place in that district, so she changed her job and now works in a factory closer to her rented house. She and her husband both had steady employment and she asked her parents to save the money they remitted from Thailand. But her parents had other uses for the money:

> I told my mother to save my money to buy a plot [of land] for my family so that one day we can come back and stay there. But my mother spent the money on her new husband's children and family. My stepfather used the money that I remitted to my mother carelessly. So, then I sent 300,000 kyats to my father and asked him to save it for me. But the same thing happened: my father's new wife and family used my money and nothing was saved for me. For us, as we stay in another country, we don't want to keep our savings here.

A number of workers told us that they had cut their ties to their families back home because they could not maintain their remittances, and they felt ashamed that their lives has not turned out as they had hoped.

Thanda Hlaing was working in Three Pagodas Pass at the time of our interview, although she had previously worked in garment factories in Mae Sot and, before that, in Yangon. After she got married she had stopped sending money home to her parents:

My parents asked me [how I am doing in Thailand]. I told them that I don't have a good income. Then they told me to come back, but I don't want to go. What I would do in Yangon? [There are] no jobs; here I have a job – I just do not have any savings. They [my parents] said they will send me money for me to come back. Then I didn't contact them again; I just gave them the phone number of a neighbour's house when I lived on the Burmese side of the border. But I did not answer when they called. So then they telephoned my employer and told him they were worried about me. I cut all contact with them for many months... They [my parents] know I am married. They will ask how much I earn and save. If I tell them I have no savings, they will ask me why I cannot save money when two people are working. Then what can I say? I don't want to let them know that my husband is a gambler... Now they know I am pregnant. They told me to come back to deliver the baby. But how can I go back? Here I can deliver [my baby] free of charge. In Burma, I have to spend money. So I won't go back.

Some migrants do make an effort to maintain their family connections, and go home for visits as often as they can. Hnin Wutyee Maw was able to buy a house in Burma, which she rented out in order to maintain a base there until the time she wants – or needs – to return:

Given the situation here, we cannot tell exactly [how long we can stay]; if they [the Thai government] say that the Burmese are not allowed to stay, we will have to go back. If I go back, I have a place to stay. If I visit, I have a place to stay. Now I rent out my house, so I earn some money.

Workers' concern over the future education of their children is another powerful factor that prevents many from leaving their jobs in Thailand in order to return home. Ye Ye Soe, a garment worker in Mae Sot, has four children, all of whom were born in Burma. She sends money to her sister back home, who takes care of the children, but the amount is far from enough to cover their needs:

I could not afford to keep my children in school at home because the costs are too high in Burma nowadays. I don't have a regular job in a factory since I quit my job a year ago, and now I earn by sewing with my own machine at my house. This is not sufficient to remit for my children's education. Although my younger sister, who is a teacher in my home town, loves my children and is willing to keep them in her school, my children don't want to stay away from me. So now they all are with me... Although my younger sister, who is single, wants to be responsible for my children's school fees because she wants her nieces to have an education, I don't want to bother her.

But it is not just the reaction of families that is decisive; workers also fear the disapproval of neighbours if they return empty-handed, with no significant savings or assets. That Yee Kyaw has been working in Three Pagodas Pass for five years. She was married two months before our interview. Her mother is also in Three Pagodas Pass; she is thinking of going back to Burma to take care of her own mother. But That Yee Kyaw herself is reluctant to return:

The money we have saved now is just enough for transportation to go back. If we go back, it will all be gone – there is nothing for us in our hometown... Our house there is now damaged. We just have some land, but we have no house to go back to and [would have to stay with the family]. I will go back only if I can build the house again... Relatives are not a problem – only neighbours [because] they will gossip. We will not have a good reputation among neighbours. Oh, they will say we have been working in another country for a long time, with no savings, no property, nothing to show for it.

Also many women and men fear that, having lived away for a long time, they will not be able to adjust to living back home again. Aung Maung is a Burman man who, unlike his wife, has never gone back to Burma in the seven years he has been working in Mae Sot.

I am a stranger in my country. Having stayed here [in Thailand] for many years, it is very difficult for me to back and stay in Burma. It is a very very difficult situation I would have to face.

Even when workers' parents put pressure on them to go back to live at home, the prospects are frequently dismal and many find that the reality of returning to Burma is unappealing. May Thu Maw came to Three Pagodas Pass four years ago, and was able to save some money, though not enough to establish a new livelihood back in Burma:

> I went back twice during Thingyan holidays. My mother did not let me come back [to Thailand]. She told me to work in my home town with them. My parents are now in their seventies. My mother saved my remittances so I could come back and establish a shop in our home town. She bought gold [for savings] for me. But the savings were not very big, and I could not find anything to do in my home town. In addition, I did not know how to use the Burmese currency. I even did not know how to live in Burma. I could not get along with the environment there. In my mind I am just thinking of working hard, earning and saving... Nothing is better than staying together with one's own family. But for survival, we have to give up our dreams and now I only want to earn good wages working hard in the factories here.

When migrants have managed to relocate their families to Thailand, their connection with home is even more tenuous. May Sabe Swe in Mae Sot explained how her family obligations, as an eldest daughter, have in the end made her shift her base to Mae Sot, resulting in her losing her home and a place to return to.

> I am the oldest daughter in the family and I have two younger brothers. Seeing my family in financial difficulties, I felt I needed to make sacrifices and start earning an income to help support my family... I decided to go to Mae Sot without my father's consent... I could not continue my schooling and left after grade 7. My father was very angry when he learned that I had gone to work in Mae Sot, but my mother understood my decision... My mother died three years ago while my brothers were still at school, so I had to become a mother to my younger brothers. Two years ago my second brother came to Mae Sot to work in the same factory as me, and my youngest brother recently joined me and is looking for a job. When my mother passed away, my father became a monk and he lives in the monastery... I sold the house in our home village as none of us was living there anymore. I don't want to be the oldest child in the family anymore; it is a big responsibility and I had to sacrifice my education for the sake of my family.

Kyaw Lin, the father of May Thin Aye, recalled how he and his wife had to come and take care of their grandchild. But they were unhappy in Mae Sot because their mobility was severely restricted as they were illegal residents. He expressed their situation in graphic terms: *hsee pu loh kone cha kha ma mee pone htel kya* (You try to jump out of the pan as the pan gets hot, but you fall onto the heated stove, which is warmer than the pan).

So many migrant workers feel that they do not have any place to return to. But as the uncertain political and economic situation continues in Thailand as well as in Burma, they fear for the future of their children as well as themselves.

> I want to send my child to study in my country. I don't have a house in my home village any more as I have sold it. But my aunts and cousins are still in the village so my child can stay with them while he is at school. I want my child to go to university. I will be very proud to see my child getting a university degree – it is a kind of dignity for my child as well... Although we are doing well here, I don't want to keep my son here for schooling – if he studies here, he will get nowhere; he could attend a migrant school but the qualifications and grades he gains may not be transferable to schools in Burma. We are not sure if the situation will allow us to stay here forever. Suppose we save enough money to start our own business in Burma and move back, it is better my child has a Burmese education. (May Sabe Swe in Mae Sot)

The situation of migrant workers in the export factories of Thailand is painful. They are unwelcome and unappreciated by their host society. They are losing their voice and their place at home, both in their families and in their communities, even though for many the prime purpose of going to Thailand to work was precisely to support their families. As the young women workers become mothers they are torn between their past – their families and the places they grew up in – and their futures and the futures of their new families. But they can only continue in this way whilst they are young and strong enough to work under the difficult conditions prevailing in the factories. After that – who knows?

When I came to Mae Sot, I had one big aim: I wanted to earn money and save so that I could invest in a stall in the Theingyizay market [a big market in Yangon selling all kinds of food, and both domestically produced and imported consumer goods]. I worked hard, morning until night, with overtime every day. I did not spend money, often going without food if I needed to buy clothes. I managed to save enough to buy a gold neckchain and one gold ring. But after working day and night continuously for three years I got sick. My knees were painful, my back ached and I had to stop sewing. I could not work for two months, and I had to sell most of my gold and use up my savings just to survive while I had no wages coming in. (Sandar Aye of Mae Sot)

7

Burmese migrant workers
between two worlds

This book has sought to illuminate the lives and struggles of
Burmese migrant workers who are employed in ready-made garment and knitting factories in present-day Thailand. As we have
explained, Thai government policy following the Asian financial
crisis in 1997 supported the decentralisation of industry, particularly to lower wages in border areas, providing a catalyst for
the recruitment of migrant workers, especially from neighbouring Burma. The two countries share a long history and a long
border. Hostile relations between the two countries date back to
the sixteenth century when Burmese imperial forces invaded the
Kingdom of Siam through Three Pagodas Pass, one of our study
areas. In recent times, historical conflicts were exacerbated in
the 1970s when Burmese socialist 'guerrillas' were accused of
supporting the student-led revolt in Thailand, which seriously
challenged the military government. Since that time Burma's
socialist state has been transformed into a repressive authoritarian
regime ruled by an increasingly hard-line military junta. Many of
the people now involved in the establishment and organisation of
diasporic schools and clinics are the same young people who as
students and intellectuals were involved in the 1988 uprising and

subsequent struggles for democracy in Burma, hence the popular moniker of 'students' clinic' given to the Mae Tao Clinic in Mae Sot directed by Dr Cynthia Maung. Exiles are also responsible for the establishment of a number of the organisations now working to defend the rights of migrant workers in the factories, fields and building sites in Thailand, as well as documenting and denouncing the ongoing human rights abuses in Burma. This makes the Thai government suspicious of such organisations and strengthens its desire to paint them as subversive and dedicated to causing political unrest in Thailand as well as in Burma.

The Pheu Thai Party, which was elected in Thailand on 11 July 2011, is effectively a reincarnation of the Thai Rak Thai Party led by the former prime minister and present fugitive Thaksin Shinawatra. The current leader of this party and the elected prime minister is Thaksin's younger sister Yingluck Shinawatra, which has led to concerns that the exiled former statesman is the real source of policy direction and power. The political terrain is complicated; the red shirts, who engaged in pitched battles with the royalist yellow shirts (who paved the way for the previous government to gain power), feel immense loyalty to Thaksin and his party.[1] These party supporters have been less concerned with the huge fortunes some politicians have amassed, allegedly the result of widespread and endemic corruption in the former regime. Rather, the historically neglected rural population have responded enthusiastically to the new political significance that Thaksin has granted them, and value highly the populist policies enacted by his government, including the introduction of universal health care. Political commentators and academics at the Thai Studies conference held in Bangkok at the end of July 2011 characterised Thaksin as a 'successful' but 'democratically primitive' politician.[2] He is seen as a pragmatic politician rather than an ideologue, who managed to woo the rural electorate whilst staunchly supporting business interests, including the expanding of investment and trade deals with Thailand's neighbouring countries in the region, including Burma. It was during Thaksin's administration that the industrial decentralisation policies were developed, result-ing in the growth of manufacturing industry in the border areas and increased cross-border trade. Between 2001 and 2006 his government also extended the period of registration for temporary migrant workers, so there is speculation within Thai business and other circles that the new government might continue the same kind of policies.

At the same time ongoing geopolitical interests in the region make it extremely unlikely that the rights and protection of migrant workers will be extended in the near future. According to a recent UNCTAD report, Thailand is likely to remain as a regional production centre for the ready-made garment and knit-wear sector. UNCTAD predicts that manufacturers from Malaysia are likely to move to Thailand 'to capitalise on this country's modern technology and abundant and more accessible skilled labour and raw materials, all of which have been important in developing the industry's local supply chain' (*Bangkok Post*, 27 July 2011). Although there is no official acknowledgement of the role of migrant workers in this 'skilled' labour force, it is very probable that the continued success of Thailand as the regional garment production hub will be underscored by access to cheap labour from its poorer neighbours.

But industry interests are not necessarily supportive of the proposed policies of the new government. The victorious Pheu Thai Party has indicated that it will implement a pre-election promise to increase the minimum wage to 300 baht across all provinces, which will effectively double the rate in low-wage areas such as Tak Province. This proposal has received a cautious welcome by commentators and labour organisations. Lae Dilokwitthayarat, a renowned economist and an expert on labour affairs, noted that local wages have been suppressed to attract investment, but in turn have increased inequality in society.[3] However, as Jackie Pollock, the director of the MAP Foundation, has pointed out, this will probably not bring much benefit to migrant workers unless the government takes on the responsibility to make sure that all workers are actually paid the full minimum wage. Given the record of industrialists in Thailand of finding mechanisms to pay migrants well below the legal minimum, there is not much optimism that the proposed change will trickle down to them.[4]

July 2011 saw the advent of another registration scheme for migrant workers, alongside the nationality verification scheme that had been introduced the previous year in line with the MOUs the Thai government signed with the three countries on its border. This process has met with the approval of employers' organisations, although the actual number of migrant workers registering under the new procedures has been lower than anticipated. Wandee Seebua-iam of the Foreign Workers' Employers Club considers that the new arrangements are in the interests of migrant workers because they hold out the promise of flexibility for those wishing to change their job during the registration period, arguing that 'registered foreign workers with work permits would have more job opportunities'.[5] However, Somkiat Chayasriwong, the permanent secretary of labour in the outgoing government, has dashed hopes that the new regime would give workers this kind of option. On 21 July 2011 he announced that 'foreign migrant workers who have registered their employment may not switch jobs. Changing employers would automatically invalidate their work permits.'[6] This stricter interpretation of the regulation appears to be a reflection of the concerns of employers in provincial areas that foreign workers once registered might leave their jobs to work in a higher paying area. With reports that migrant workers are being poached to work in central areas, where wages are higher, employers are concerned to retain control over the registered workers in their factories, arguing that the relatively low number of migrant workers who have completed the registration process means that they will have no option but to employ unregistered migrants if those with documentation move to higher-paying jobs. This is far from the public objective of the government, which is that once migrant workers have obtained their temporary passports and work permits they will enjoy the same rights and entitlements as Thai workers.

This double standard is also reflected in the new Private Insurance Scheme for Migrant Workers, which was established in the summer of 2010. Under this scheme employers are advised that they have the option to buy private insurance for migrant workers at a cost of 500 baht each, to cover compensation in the event of workplace accidents. But, unlike the Workmen's Compensation Fund, which is hosted by the Social Security Office and is compulsory and legally enforceable, the new scheme is optional and therefore not legally binding on employers, and inevitably means that migrant workers are not insured against workplace accidents and injuries.[7]

The ways in which the new government chooses to control migrant workers, without choking off the supply of cheap labour for Thai employers, remains to be seen. Certainly there are signs that the government will seek better relations with its neighbours. There were serious border clashes between Thailand and Cambodia in 2011, which led to a request by the International Court of Justice for Thai troops to withdraw from occupied territory and temples. Smarn Lertwongrath, an adviser to the Pheu Thai Party, has given the impression that Thailand would become a better neighbour under the new government. He believes that 'borders are very out of date... they are no longer an issue with globalization' and that Thailand, one of the founder nations of ASEAN, would be keen to seek a solution under its auspices.[8]

However, Thailand's relations with Cambodia continue to be influenced by access to oil and gas reserves in disputed areas of the Gulf of Thailand. Similar economic and geopolitical issues also underline relations between Thailand and Burma, not least because Burma's extensive reserves of gas and oil have made it the major supplier of energy to Thailand, a position it is set to assume also for Yunnan province in China. Australian economist Sean Turnell estimates that Burmese gas fields are expected to produce 540 million cubic metres and generate $3-5 billion per year for the next thirty years.[9] The paradox of Burma in economic terms is that it is totally viable in terms of international economic relations, but that this relative prosperity has not changed the grinding poverty in which most of the population, especially in the rural areas, still live. Little of the government's wealth is spent on social sectors, with far less being directed to education and health, whilst the military is well catered for. Inflation is rampant, estimated at over 30 per cent per year. And the recent appreciation of the country's currency, apparently based on the increase in drug exports undertaken to finance border-area insurgencies, puts the Burmese economy on a positive footing. This contrasts with the historic devaluation that took place over the previous two decades, and has aided the recovery in Burma's external balance of payments. But it has made life even harder for those who depend on remittances from family members abroad.[10]

Expectations of political reform were heightened by the elections held in Burma in November 2010, which have given the country a nominally civilian government. Initially the National League for Democracy opted to boycott the election due to the restrictive terms of political participation allowed, leaving much of the country without any real democratic choice. Aung San Suu Kyi was released in November 2010, an act welcomed by the people of Burma and the international community. This may herald the promise of a cautious move towards genuine reform.

In the summer of 2011 there were reports of increased violations of human rights; the Burmese military were alleged to be using prison inmates as human shields in minesweeping exercises, and executing those who tried to escape. Both Poe Shan, director of the Burma-based Karen Human Rights Group, and Elaine Pearson, deputy Asia director of US-based Human Rights Watch, warned European governments and ASEAN countries against hoping for things magically to improve in Burma, urging that there should be a UN commission of inquiry to investigate human rights abuses in the country. A further disturbing element was the reports from various quarters in July 2011 of systematic rape being deployed as a military tactic against rebel communities in Kachin and Shan states.[11] These developments, together with an apparent escalation in the involvement of armed opposition groups in drug production and export in order to raise funds for military activity, appear to presage an intensification of conflict within the country rather than a progressive move to political openness and democracy.

Nevertheless, by autumn 2011 some limited progressive measures had been introduced by the Burmese government, including the release of a small number of high-profile political prisoners in September 2011. Aung San Suu Kyi gave a guarded welcome to changes which she said provide a basis for optimism about the possibility of a return to democracy. The Burmese government's decision to suspend the construction of the Myitsone Dam until at least 2015, which was supposed to be built with Chinese investment, was seen as a change in attitude in the face of widespread opposition from civil society. In November 2011 Aung San Suu Kyi announced that she intended to be one of the NLD candidates to contest forthcoming elections for forty-eight parliamentary seats, reflecting a growing confidence in the present political setup. Meanwhile a number of high-profile Western government representatives, including Hillary Clinton (USA), William Hague (UK) and Nicolas Sarkozy (France) have paid visits to Burma and met with members of the ruling junta.

However, it will take a long time for the economic prospects of ordinary people in Thailand to improve substantially. Meanwhile the devastating floods have hit many workplaces hard, including factories that employ Burmese migrant workers. With poor Thai-language skills, many migrants found it difficult to access accurate information or relief efforts, and many remained trapped for prolonged periods of time or were forced to return home. And, as ever, arrest and extortion by police and others served to exacerbate an already grim situation.[12]

In the meantime, as this book makes clear, migrant workers from Burma working in the export factories of Thailand are literally suspended between two worlds. The civic infrastructure, economic opportunity, education and health systems of Burma, where they spent their early years and attended school, have systematically deteriorated. It would be wrong to assume that the migrant workers in the ready-made garment and knitwear factories in Thailand are from the 'poorest of the poor' within Burmese society; like migrants in other contexts, these people come from families which have been able to raise the funds to pay for the expenses of migration – either by liquidating family assets or borrowing, or from remittances of previous migrant family members. Nor are they drawn from the group of mainly ethnic minorities in Burma who have been the long-standing object of forced displacement and atrocities by the SPDC armed forces, who have razed villages, destroyed crops, kidnapped young people for forced labour, and abused and raped women and girls.[13] Many of this group are stranded in the camps for displaced people that line the Western border between Thailand and Burma. They are often stuck there for years awaiting the opportunity to settle in a third country, since Thailand is not a signatory of the 1951 UN Convention on Refugees, and does not itself offer the possibility of permanent settlement or citizenship.

The migrant workers in our study are relatively well educated, and generally from families which have seen better days; families that have lived through the progressive deterioration of the hard-won gains of Burmese independence, not least the quality of schools and universities, hospitals and clinics. Caught between these two worlds, of the past and the present, they have turned to migration as a family strategy to save themselves from falling even further into desperation and hopelessness. Their relatively sound education has taught them that there are better opportunities elsewhere; and whilst the older generation usually feel that they are too old and inexperienced to travel in search of work, their children are ready to do so on their own as well as their families' behalf, even though – like migrants all over the world – the actual employment available to them is well below what they might expect in other circumstances, given their education and social status.

Women in particular live the contradictions of this suspension between different worlds. As we have seen, most arrive in Thailand at a relatively young age, often having had no experience of living independently. During their time in Thailand they gain experience; they learn to negotiate the particular factory regimes in which they are inserted, with a greater or lesser degree of success. They learn to live more or less independently, or at least to depend on a much wider circle of relatives and friends than the nuclear family structure in which they had been constrained and sheltered in Burma. In Thailand most have had to operate in an alien society and language, although, as we have seen, some were able to shelter in a Burmese-speaking bubble of house factories and dormitories. They have had to pick their way through a complex and changing situation of regulation and registration, often relying on word of mouth and rumour to learn about new decrees and policies, especially when they lack contact with support organisations, and no comprehension of Thai-language newspapers or other sources of news. They also have learned the hidden scripts of such regulation; the fact that in many situations it suits the employer as well as the worker not to comply with registration procedures, but to collude to work for lower wages and worse conditions as unregistered migrants.

This offers an ideal and flexible workforce to an industry struggling to remain competitive and viable in a world economy rocked by successive crises and living in the shadow of the burgeoning Chinese economy, which is proving to be a more efficient and lower-wage source of the very export goods Thailand has long relied on to earn foreign exchange. They have to learn to navigate a legal and institutional system where all is not as it seems; where the authorities charged with enforcing the law and protecting people from abuse are often the very same institutions that violate the law, inflicting harassment, arbitrary arrest, bribes, and fines on unprotected workers, and where the collusion between the border authorities in both countries implies frequent deportation, always involving payment as well as other abuses.

Given their age at the time of migration, it is hardly surprising that many factory workers begin families of their own once they are working in Thailand. And, as we have seen, it is at this point in their life course that the full implications of their trans-border identities begin to be played out. The range of issues discussed here – whether they should have children, whether to continue or terminate a pregnancy, where to give birth, how to organise care for infants without losing their job, how to look after older children and ensure appropriate schooling, whether to keep the children with them in Thailand or send them home to the family in Burma, how to combine their new responsibilities as wives and mothers with their ongoing obligations to parents and other relatives – are the practical matters that shape the women's lives. Underlying them is a whole other range of challenges. How does a woman worker, married with small children, maintain links to her family and community back home? How often can she take the risk, or afford, to visit them? Should she insist that her children are brought up as Burmese or allow them to integrate with the local population in Thailand?

The question of the citizenship status of the workers and their children is ever present, and has recently become more acute with the introduction of a nationality verification requirement as part of the registration regulations under the MOU between Thailand and Burma. But the acquisition of this nationality document – which is not really a passport because it is not valid for any journey other than crossing overland between Burma and Thailand for the purposes of registering as an irregular worker – carries costs as well as risks to the families still living at home. More significantly, under this system there is no provision for the establishment of the nationality of children and other family members of migrant workers. The estimated 50,000 children per year born to migrant workers in Thailand are largely without official citizenship in either Burma or Thailand, a situation which threatens their educational future, and their ability to participate in democratic and civil political activity. As the economic and political relationship between the two countries, at the level of ASEAN and other international bodies and treaties, grows stronger, the prospect of resolving this issue and improving the present and future position of migrant workers grows ever more unlikely.

This situation leaves hundreds of thousands of migrant workers with an ongoing dilemma. They have devoted several years of their lives to working in factories and elsewhere, earning a wage that is generally below the legally stipulated rate for their work but one that makes a significant difference to their survival and that of their families. When they have to make decisions about the immediate and more long-term future, particularly concerning their children, they are forced to do so on the basis of uncertainty both about what is likely to happen in their home country and regarding what the future might offer in Thailand. And, as we have indicated above, the immediate direction of travel of both countries is not positive. At present we are witnessing an increase in the surveillance and restriction of migrant workers in Thailand as much for political as for other reasons. But industrialists continue to demand access to cheap migrant workers. And in spite of the apparently positive recent changes in Burma, there is little sign of an economic revival or of extensive political liberalisation under the present regime.

In this climate the choices women make are often pragmatic and short term, driven by economic survival. But, as our interviews reveal, women also have dreams for the future. They are willing to make sacrifices for their children, just as their parents were willing to allow them to leave the discipline of their family structure to migrate to a strange and distant location in order to earn money and support the whole family. Present-day migrant workers in Thailand are intent on maintaining that economic role, but at the same time organising the care and schooling of their children in a manner which keeps options for future education and citizenship open, depending on what opportunities arise. But in doing this they are frequently sacrificing themselves for their families' future. Many dream of returning home with sufficient capital to buy assets and businesses which might insulate them and their families against economic stagnation and decline in Burma.

But they know in their heart of hearts that this kind of economic activity depends on a degree of revival and renewal in the Burmese economy that might provide the consumer or industrial demand for the products and services of their businesses, and that this does not seem very likely at the present time. It is true that there is an increase in trans-border investment and trade between Burma and Thailand and other countries in the Greater Mekong Subregion, but this is not necessarily trickling down to the level of small enterprises and local employment; rather, the main opportunities are for state-owned corporations, or joint venture companies in which the military are generally the Burmese partner; little of the increased revenues translate into enhanced consumption income for ordinary people.

But what are these women to do? Their experiences as migrant workers have changed them, and they frequently feel hesitant about returning to where they came from, having achieved a level of autonomy and self-reliance in Thailand as the result of their deter-mination and hard work. They cannot assume things will improve at home, and for many the changes in their family circumstances since they came to Thailand may mean that their priority is now securing an alternative future for their children. But the ongoing marginalisation and hostility they face from officialdom and from the general Thai population continue, conspiring with the appetite of Thai industrialists for cheap flexible labour to maintain their invisibility and voicelessness. This book is intended to give a voice to some of the migrant women from Burma who are working in Thailand's factories.

There are perhaps a few – minor – developments that might give some hope for positive change. There is certainly greater international awareness of the situation in Burma, because of ongoing political mobilisation by exile and diaspora communi-ties, not just in neighbouring Asian countries but also in North America, Australia, New Zealand and Europe. where refugees under the protection of the United Nations High Commissioner for Refugees (UNHCR) have been welcomed and settled. The recent

BBC Reith Lectures[14] by Aung San Suu Kyi, concerning democracy and political change, were broadcast to dozens of countries across the world. Thai unions and labour organisations have substantially changed their opposition to migrant workers, and are cooperating more effectively with Burmese and other migrant organisations. The organisations themselves have gained in experience and effectiveness, and frequently participate in UN and other international forums on migration and rights of migrant workers. The sharp increase in migration in all regions of the global economy has focused attention on the issue of rights and protection of migrant workers, which has served to legitimate the struggles of Burmese migrant labour. However, for the foreseeable future it is unlikely that the women and men working in Thailand's factories and other enclaves of cheap and unprotected workers will experience any improvement in their rights and conditions.

> By analysing women's narratives of themselves and others, we can allow them to explicate and account for their lives and situations, the terms in which they act and are reacted to, and thereby uncover the loci of their interests and action.[15]

As this book goes to press the Burmese state is in a state of transition after the new constitution and general election of 2011, and the more recent election of Aung San Suu Kyi and forty-two other members of her National League for Democracy to parliament in April 2012. However, it is not anticipated that there will be any rapid changes to alter the situation fundamentally for Burmese migrant workers in Thailand.

APPENDIX ONE

History of registration exercises for irregular (temporary) migrant workers

1ST REGISTRATION ROUND
(25 June 1996 cabinet resolution)
- November 1996–August 1998
- Two-year permit
- Migrant and employer report to immigration every 3 months
- 43 of 72 provinces for 11 sectors
- Introduction of a category of 'temporary resident permit while awaiting deportation' (Tor Mor 69)

2ND REGISTRATION ROUND
- August 1998–August 1999
- One-year permit
- 37 provinces, 18 category of manual labour
- Permit border commuters

3RD REGISTRATION ROUND
(4 August 1999 cabinet resolution)
- August 1999–August 2000
- One-year permit
- 7 provinces, 18 types of work

4TH REGISTRATION ROUND
 (29 August 2000 cabinet resolution)
- September 2000–August 2001
- 37 provinces, 18 sectors.
- Pregnancy testing as condition for deportation

5TH REGISTRATION ROUND
 (28 August 2001 cabinet resolution)
- September 2001–February 2002
- Six-month permits renewable for a further six months
- All types of manual labour
- Registration without employer (to be found within 6 months)
- Inclusion of domestic workers
- Health check-up after 6 months

COMPLETION OF 5TH REGISTRATION ROUND
- March 2002–August 2002
- Six months renewal
- If 5th registration round completed and if employer found, one-year permit provided (August 2002–July 2003)
- Change of employer only allowed if with papers from previous and prospective employers
- Firms with BOI not allowed to employ alien workers

RE-REGISTRATION RELATED TO 5TH REGISTRATION ROUND
- August 2003–August 2004
- One-year permit
- Only migrants registered in 2001 and re-registered in 2002

6TH REGISTRATION ROUND
 (27 April 2004 cabinet resolution)
- July 2004–June 2005
- One-year permit
- Application for temporary ID card (Tor Ror 38/1) at district level, independent of employer (can apply without employer)

- Registration for work permit with employer
- Mobility limited to place of employment
- Medical check

RE-REGISTRATION RELATED TO 6TH REGISTRATION ROUND
(10 May 2005 cabinet resolution)
- July 2005–June 2006
- One-year permit
- Migrants who acquired an ID card in 2004 able to register for the first time with employer
- Re-registration of migrants who had registered with employer
- Border provinces could make arrangements for cross-border seasonal workers

RE-REGISTRATION RELATED TO 6TH REGISTRATION ROUND
(20 December 2006 cabinet resolution)
- March 2006–February 2007
- One-year permit
- Only re-registration
- Introduced deposit fee (50,000 baht for new arrivals, 10,000 baht for previously registered)

RE-REGISTRATION RELATED TO 6TH REGISTRATION ROUND
(18 May 2006 cabinet resolution)
- July 2006–June 2007
- One-year permit
- Only migrants registered in 2004 who had maintained the registration able to register

RE-REGISTRATION RELATED TO 6TH REGISTRATION ROUND
(19 December 2006 cabinet resolution)
- March 2007–February 2008 and July 2007–June 2008
- One-year permit
- Only migrants who previously registered able to re-register

RE-REGISTRATION RELATED TO 6TH REGISTRATION ROUND
  (18 December 2007 cabinet resolution)
- March 2008-
- One-year permit, renewable for 2 year

RE-REGISTRATION RELATED TO 6TH REGISTRATION ROUND
- July 2008-
- One-year permit, renewable for 2 years

7TH REGISTRATION ROUND
  (26 May 2009 cabinet resolution)
- July 2009-February 2010
- Nationality verification process
- Process of nationality verification process for Burmese migrants implemented from 15 July 2009
- MOU was signed in June 2003

EXTENSION OF 7TH REGISTRATION ROUND
  (19 January 2010 cabinet resolution)
- February 2010-February 2012
- Those who register must apply for nationality verification process by 28 February 2010
- Deadline to complete nationality verification process extended to 28 February 2012 for those who registered and obtained work permit in 2009

Sources Sciortino and Punpuing 2009; IOM Migration information note Issue #4 February 2010; IOM Migration information note August 2009; Mekong Migration Network Migrant registration in Thailand: Timeline of facts and figures, www. mekongmigration.org/PDF%20for%20policy%20documents/Diagram_Registration %20in%20Thailand_2.pdf; accessed 27 October 2011.

APPENDIX TWO

Currency exchange rates:
Thai baht/Burmese kyat/US dollar

Since 2001 the official exchange rate has been between 5.75 and 6.70 kyat to US$1, but the black-market rate, listed below from 1997 to May 2011, more accurately takes into account the national economy.

	US$ as	
	Burmese kyat	Thai baht
January–December 1997	167–257	25.6–42.3
End 2000	435	43.8
January–December 2004	815–970	40.0
End 2005	1075	41.3
February 2007	1280	35.1
March 2008	1100	31.5
August 2009	1130	34.0
October 2010	890	30.2
May 2011	823	30.0

For kyat official exchange rates 1997–2005, see www.nationsencyclopedia.com/economies/Asia-and-the-Pacific/Burma-Myanmar-money.html.

Notes

CHAPTER I

1. Burma is the name for the country used since British colonial rule. However, the country was renamed by the ruling military government as the Union of Myanmar in 1989 and in 2011 the Republic of the Union of Myanmar. The name remains contested. The UN has endorsed the name Myanmar, although many Western governments still refer to the country as Burma. Media outlets have a mixed practice. Opposition groups, especially non-Burman ethnic groups, refuse to recognise the new name because the term 'Myanmar' has historically been used to refer to the majority Burman ethnic group. Our practice is to retain the name 'Burma', which is common among migrant workers in Thailand, and in the English-speaking media and academia, but we use Burma/Myanmar when we refer to official treaties or government actions.
2. Razavi 1999.
3. Pollock and Aung 2010; McCarthy 2010; Fink 2009.
4. 'Race to the bottom' refers to employers reducing costs at the expense of workers. Moreover, the lack of focus on social and environmental standards often results in job losses or inadequate working conditions for the workers. For the literature on exploitation of Burmese migrant workers, see Yimprasert and Hveem 2005; Arnold and Hewison 2005.
5. Martin 2007: 4; Human Rights Watch 2010.
6. According to Human Rights Watch (2010: 8), migrant workers account for between 5 and 10 per cent of the workforce in Thailand.
7. According to the UN Refugee Agency (UNHCR), Thailand currently hosts 96,800 refugees from Myanmar (Burma) who have been registered, and an estimated 53,000 who have not and are living in nine government-

run camps along the 1,400 km Thai-Burmese border. See www.unhcr.
org/4cd970109.html.

8. Details about the history of Burma can be found in Fink 2009. Although
the scene of long intra-ethnic and colonial wars, Burma emerged in the
1960s as a potentially stable and progressive country, offering employment and a decent living standard to its increasingly educated and healthy
population. But a series of military coups have transformed the country
into an isolated and degenerative state, tolerated by its Asian neighbours
in the name of regional security, and because of the oil and other natural
resources it offers to internationals investors.

9. According to *The Times* online, astrologers and soothsayers have advised
the Burmese government on building the new capital. See www.timeson-
line.co.uk/tol/news/world/article587790.ece.

10. Fink 2009; McCarthy 2010.

11. Rangoon is the old colonial name of the former capital of Burma/Myan-
mar, now known as Yangon. Although the military government officially
relocated the capital to Naypyidaw in March 2006, Yangon, with a population of over 4 million, continues to be the country's largest city and the
most important commercial centre.

12. Because of the government's reluctance to allow foreigners into the
country, UN and international NGOs were given only very belated and
restricted access to the disaster areas, with international aid often being
sequestered and diverted by the military. http://news.bbc.co.uk/2/hi/
uk_news/politics/7396313.stm; www.siiaonline.org/ ?q=programmes/
insights/myanmar-cyclone-nargis-aid-still-needed-maybe-misused.

13. Seekins 2009.

14. According to the ILO (2007), there was a ninefold wage gap between
Thailand and Burma in 2007 and rising.

15. The first garment factory in Three Pagodas Pass began production in 1996.
Since then there has been a rapid expansion of factories, including in 1996
the establishment of a large-scale factory producing footwear (trainers)
for a global brand. Mosquito nets for UN humanitarian programmes are
also produced here with a 100 per cent Burmese labour force.

16. The research was carried out by Burmese Karen researchers who stayed
for extensive periods. The life histories of 133 Burmese migrant workers
(107 women and 26 men) were constructed, and a structured questionnaire survey of a total of 504 migrant workers was carried out. All of the
names of the respondents quoted are pseudonyms in order to maintain
their anonymity.

17. The gender composition of the migrant labour force in Thailand's establishments is difficult to estimate.

18. Yeates 2009.

19. Shafaeddin 2004.

20. Elson and Pearson 1981; Joekes 1987.

21. Skill is deemed to be innate rather than acquired through experience
and training, and is thus not taken into account in the setting of wages.

For the literature on cheap and docile Third World women workers, see Elson and Pearson 1981.

22. Pearson 1995.
23. Barrientos 2007.
24. UN–INSTRAW (UN Women) 2007.
25. Pearson and Seyfang 2001.
26. Kojima 2007.
27. Davin 1998.
28. Ngai 2005.
29. This is elaborated in detail in Pearson and Kusakabe 2012, forthcoming.
30. Human Rights Watch 2010: 19.
31. This is the title of the 2010 *Human Rights Report* on the abuse of migrant workers in Thailand; it is based on a Thai proverb.
32. The National Building period in the 1940s, which consolidated the modern state of Thailand (originally the old Kingdom of Siam), elevated ethnic Thais as the only legitimate indigeneity of the country, marginalising other (more long-standing) peoples in the country. For more information on hill tribes and nationalities, see Gillogly 2004; MAP Foundation n.d.
33. MAP Foundation n.d.
34. Thawdar, 'No Country to Call Their Own', *Irawaddy*, vol. 17, no. 5, August 2009, www.irrawaddy.org/article.php?art_id=16438.
35. Usa Pichai, 'Thailand Promises Equal Education to All Children', *Mizzima*, 13 June 2009, www.mizzima.com/news/regional/2297-thailand-promises-equal-education-to-all-children.html.
36. Hochschild 2000: 131.
37. Yeates 2009.
38. Fröbel et al. 1980.
39. Stratton, 'Burma Referendum Begins while Aid Trickles in', *Guardian*, 10 May 2008, www.guardian.co.uk/world/2008/may/10/burma.naturaldisasters.
40. Burma is seeking to play a more active role in the region and has made a bid to chair ASEAN in 2014, which has focused the minds of other governments on human rights and democracy issues in the country. See http://democracyforburma.wordpress.com/2011/05/15/political-situation-in-burma-needs-to-improve/.
41. For The Economist Intelligence Unit on Thailand, see http://country.eiu.com/Thailand; and 'Thailand Political and Economic Outlook 2011 and Beyond', http://hubpages.com/hub/Thailand-Political-and-Economic-Outlook-2011-and-Beyond.

CHAPTER 2

1. Harada and Yasuhisa 1998.
2. For a detailed account of the political and economic policies underlying Thailand's industrialisation in the twentieth century, see Somboon Siripra-

chai, 'Industrialisation and Inequality in Thailand', http://econ.tu.ac.th/ archan/rangsun/ec%20460/ec%20460%20readings/thai%20economy/ Industrialization/Industrialsation%20and%20Inequality%20in%20Thai land.pdf; Suehiro 2000.

3. Phongpaichit and Baker 1998: 133.
4. 'Thailand – Labor', www.nationsencyclopedia.com/Asia-and-Oceania/ Thailand-LABOR.html#ixzz1MCS9tJm4.
5. Phongphaichit and Baker 1998.
6. ESCAP 2003: 67.
7. ILO 2002: 35.
8. A series of employment-creation measures were introduced with an external injection of funds through Miyazawa Plan (US$1.45 billion), World Bank (US$60 million), Japan Exim Bank (US$600 million) and OECF (US$250 million).
9. Behrman et al. 2001.
10. Hicken 2008.
11. Chalamwong and Amornthum 2002.
12. This is discussed in detail in Kusakabe and Pearson 2010.
13. 'Supply Chain in Thai Garment Industry: Impact on women workers!', Thai Labour Campaign/Oxfam, www.scribd.com/doc/36259011/Supply-Chain-in-Thai-Garment-Industry-Impact-on-women-workers 2003.
14. The Bagan declaration envisages the development of sister city relation-ships between Myawaddy and Mae Sot, Thachilek and Mae Sai, Koh Song and Ranong, Phaya Thone Zu and Three Pagodas Pass, Dawei and Kanchanaburi, Bokypin and Bang Sapan, Kyaing Tong and Chiang Rai, Mandalay and Chiang Mai, Yangon and Bangkok.
15. Office of the National Economic and Social Development Board 2003.
16. Tsuneishi 2005: 7.
17. Special economic zones were originally proposed for cities at the border and along the Greater Mekon Subregion economic corridors – the cross-border highways that cut across countries in the Mekong.
18. See www.ipetitions.com/petition/support_thai_migrant_workers/. Con-trols on and harassment of migrant workers are reported to be increasing; see www.burmanet.org/news/2011/04/06/irrawaddy-thai-police-oppres-sion-for-burmese-untouchables-%E2%80%93-ba-kaung; accessed 7 June 2011.
19. *Bangkok Post*, 5 July 2010.
20. *Bangkok Post*, 18 May 2009.
21. This is detailed in Chapter 3.
22. Chalamwong and Amornthum 2002: 15.
23. *Bangkok Post*, 7 October 2009.
24. Skeldon 1999.
25. Phongpaichit and Baker 2000: 178-9.
26. Traitongyoo 2008.
27. www.asiaobserver.com/Burma/Burma-background-economy.htm.
28. *Bangkok Post*, 30 January 2009.

29. Sciortino and Punpuing 2009.
30. Sciortino and Punpuing 2009: 23.
31. Martin 2007: 5.
32. Martin et al. 2004: 22.
33. For more on birth control, see Chapter 5.
34. Map Foundation website.
35. For details and up-to-date information on the current status of registration and the application of the MOU 'passport' and work permit system, see the MAP Foundation website: www.mapfoundationcm.org; also www.nationmultimedia.com/2011/05/04/opinion/Migration-management-in-Thailand-reaches-acrossro-30154495.html.
36. According to the TDRI, if the migrant population decreased by 480,000, wages of Thai workers would only increase by 1.1 per cent, but migrant wage levels would be driven up by 40.3 per cent. An increase of 100,000 in the numbers of migrant works (equivalent to 10 per cent of the estimated number currently in Thailand) would reduce migrant wages by 11 per cent but only lead to a 0.25 per cent fall in Thai wages.
37. *Bangkok Post*, 26 June 2007.
38. Some studies and reports reinforce prejudice against migrant workers. For example, Pornthipsathern's (2003) study confirmed the hypothesis that foreign workers who are young, male, on a low income, working long hours, in units with many other workers have a higher tendency to cause social problems, without a careful comparison with Thais from a similar background working in comparable conditions.
39. ODI 2011.

CHAPTER 3

1. A number of studies have been conducted by NGOs, both Thai and Burmese, and academic institutions on the situation of migrant factory workers in Thailand: World Vision and ARCM 2003, Institute of Asian Studies et al. 2003; Thammasak 1998; FTUB and Robertson Jr 2006; Hveem and Doke 2004; Pearson et al. 2006; ARCM et al. 2004; Pollock 2006s.
2. Caouette et al. 2006.
3. FTUB and Robertson Jr. 2006.
4. MAP Foundation (website) reports that only 27,253 Burmese workers renewed their registration in June 2006 in Tak Province, showing a large reduction in the number of registered migrant workers, because most workers were not able to re-register.
5. Data downloaded from www.irrawaddy.org/bur/index.php/news/1-news/3138-2010-05-11-12-55-08). Also see Chapter 4 for details.
6. See Chapter 1 n11 above.
7. See Theobald 2001.
8. According to Pattanarak Foundation researchers, whom we interviewed in 2008, and Saw Yan Naing, 'Economic Slowdown Hits Burmese Migrant

Workers in Thailand', *Irrawady News*, 28 November 2008, there are around 13,000 workers in Three Pagodas Pass.

9. The respondents and research team frequently refer to this location as 'Bangkok' due to its proximity to the capital.

10. 'As of February 2011 87% of the registered migrants were from Burma': Office of Foreign Workers Administration, Bangkok, http://wp.doe. go.th/executive-summary; accessed 25 October 2011.

11. According to the NSO website (accessed June 2007), in 2006 there were 1,093 registered establishments in Samut Prakan province employing 121,915 people. According to Sciortino and Punpuing 2009, there were 20,120 registered migrant workers in Samut Prakan in 2007.

12. www.newsclip/be/news/2009107_022076.html.

13. Sciortino and Punpuing 2009: 64.

14. There are extensive reports of forced relocation of slum residents and others around Yangon. See www.ibiblio.org/obl/docs4/Rangoon-docs. pdf.

15. IOM 2005; Nwe 2003; Hayami 2004.

16. According to Turnell et al. (2010) *'hundi* is an ancient device in which monetary value is transferred via a network of dealers or brokers from one location to another'; known as *hawala* in the Arabic-speaking world, *chiao hui* in China, and *poey kwan* in Thailand.

17. These are different from the agents who arrange migrants' journeys to and employment in Thailand.

18. By the sixth year, more than half of the male migrants had stopped remitting, compared to less than 40 per cent of the women (Turnell et al. 2010).

19. Lee 1998, quoting Margaret Somers (1994: 624).

CHAPTER 4

1. These are factories located along the river that demarcate the border between Thailand and Burma. They are situated away from the town of Mae Sot itself, concentrated together near an informal border crossing. They normally pay lower wages than in other Mae Sot factories, but, on the other hand, there are fewer checks by the authorities.

2. See Office of Foreign Workers Administration website, http://wp.doe. go.th/sites/default/files/statistic/9/se03-54.pdf; accessed 25 October 2011. However, these figures may be an overestimate since some workers are included in both categories (registration and nationality verification).

3. FTUB and Robertson Jr 2006.

4. Sciortino and Punpuing 2009.

5. Pattanarak Foundation, www.pattanarak.or.th; Saw Yan Naing, 'Economic Slowdown Hits Burmese Migrant Workers in Thailand', *Irrawady News*, 28 November 2008.

6. See report on the workshop: www.gender-migration.ait.ac.th/Workshop s&Field%20Research.html. For other researchers, see World Vision and

ARCM 2003; Institute of Asian Studies et al. 2003; Anchalee 1998; Arnold 2004, 2006; FTUB 2004, 2006; Amnesty International 2005; Hveem and Doke 2004; Elaine et al. 2006; Chulalongkorn University 2003; Asian Human Rights Commission 2005; ARCM et al. 2004; Caouette 2001; Huguet and Punpuing 2005; Martin 2004 et al.; Wai 2004; Pollock 2005.

7. Punpuing et al. 2006.

8. Fourteen women in our sample have dependent children living with them in Mae Sot. Among the twenty-five married women interviewed, all but three were living with their husbands in Mae Sot. All six married male respondents had wives living with them in Mae Sot.

9. Several Burmese groups support migrant workers on labour issues in Mae Sot, even though they are not formally recognised as trade unions. They have no legal status in Thailand, but tend to work closely with Thai NGOs such as MAP Foundation and Labour Law Clinic.

10. Yaung Chi Oo Workers Association website (http://yaungchioo.org downloaded on 28 July 2008) indicates that, together with MAP Foundation and the Lawyer Council of Thailand, during 2002–06 it supported 1,383 Burmese workers in Thailand in 101 cases. Few Burmese migrant workers are fortunate or courageous enough to find support and fight for their rights.

11. Punpuing et al. 2006.

12. Mekong Migration Network and Asian Migration Centre 2008.

13. Punpuing et al. 2006.

14. Arnold and Pickles 2011.

15. Arnold 2004; FTUB and Robertson Jr 2006.

16. Ibid.

CHAPTER 5

1. Interview with Dr Maung, 9 July 2007.

2. John Bercow, *Reproductive Health in Burma*, www.fmreview.org/FMRpdfs/FMR30/22-23.pdf.

3. Khom Chat Luk, 15 May 2008.

4. This table refers to the responses of 283 respondents whose first child was born after they came to Thailand. Some women had more than one child (thirty-one women in Mae Sot and eight women in Three Pagodas Pass had two children; two women in Mae Sot and two women in Three Pagodas Pass had three children).

5. Workers in Three Pagodas Pass who organised childcare on the Burmese side of the border are included in the category of 'childcare in Thailand'.

6. Caouette et al. 2006.

7. The scheme, known as the 30 Baht Universal Health Coverage Policy, was launched in 2001 by the Thaksin government. Anyone who was not covered by another health insurance scheme was given a card that

allowed them to use public health services for a payment of 30 baht per visit. In 2007 the scheme was changed to allow all Thai citizens to access public health services free of charge; however, migrant workers were still required to pay the 30 baht fee.

8. Archavanitkul 2002.

9. Ling 2007.

10. 'Advocacy for Child Protection and Education for Burmese Children', Health Sciences Centre, Calgary, 24 September 2009.

11. Supporting organisations include the Korean government, the Taipei Overseas Peace Services, the Jesuit Refugee Service, Open Society Institute, Brackett Foundation, Help Without Frontiers (Italy), Children's Dream, World Education, Human Rights Education Institute of Burma, Planet Cares.

12. www.worlded.org.

13. The project team has tried to assist some migrant children who were seeking to enter a Thai school in one of the research sites. At first the school authorities denied that there was any policy declaration that made it their duty to accept migrant children. However, the provincial education office confirmed that this was now national policy and wrote a letter of support for the children. We returned to the school with the letter, but they said there were no vacancies for the children, so they should enrol in another school. In order to enrol in that school, they said, the children needed a Thai household registration document, which as migrant workers they do not have. Then the school said that the children could ask a Thai neighbour to put the children's names in their household registration. Thus, even though the policy exists on paper, there are many obstacles to actually enrolling migrant children, and it is almost impossible for migrant parents to go through the bureaucratic process themselves.

14. Ekachai 2007.

15. Recent research by this project indicates that there was ideological resistance by teachers to accepting the children of migrant workers in their schools, in addition to the bureaucratic and financial obstacles, despite clear government policy in favour of integration.

CHAPTER 6

1. Message by Juan Somavia, director general of the International Labour Organization, on the occasion of International Migrants Day, 18 December 2008; www.ilo.org/[[ublic/english/bureau/dgo/speeches/somavia/2008/migrants.pdf.

2. McCargo 2008.

3. *The Economist*, 19 March 2009.

4. Aung and Aung 2009.

5. This is a vigilante group which the migrant workers refer to as 'the Palm Gang', so-called because they wear shirts with a picture of a palm tree

on them. They are an unofficial group of Thai men who 'volunteer' to maintain security in Mae Sot. We have no information regarding who is behind the organisation. There are stories of them capturing Burmese workers who do 'wrong' things such as stealing; and there are even suggestions of lynchings and executions. It is said that they also retain Thai nationals who commit crimes, but these they hand over to the police rather than mete out their own summary 'justice'. They appear to act with impunity and the migrant workers fear them. One story concerned a Burmese migrant worker caught stealing in the market: the Palm Gang put tyres round him and set light to them and he burned to death. However, we have no reports of the Palm Gang since 2008, and do not know if they are still operating in Mae Sot.

6. The ID card is a combination of registration and work permit.
7. *Daily News*, 30 December 2010.
8. *Khao Sot*, 20 June 2010.
9. Traitongyoo 2008.
10. *Kom Chad Leuk*, 3 March 2010.
11. *The Nation*, 23 August 2010. King Naresuan was a Thai hero during the Ayudhaya period. He defeated Burma and brought independence to the Thais.

CHAPTER 7

1. See the BBC's analysis of the red versus yellow shirt conflict: www.bbc.co.uk/news/world-asia-pacific-13294268. Others frame the confrontation as a conflict between two oligarchies, the traditional elites and the nouveau riche. See www.smh.com.au/opinion/politics/thai-turmoil-was-no-class-war-20100607-xped.html,
2. These are the words of Craig Reynolds, an Australian expert on Thai politics and history, spoken during the 11th International Conference on Thai Studies, 26-28 July 2011, Mahidol University, Bangkok.
3. *Bangkok Post*, 26 July 2011, www.bangkok post.com/news/politics/248781/academics-support-wage-rise-proposal; accessed 25 October 2011.
4. http://ap-irnet.ilobkk.or.th/news/thailand-poor-foreign-workers-no-minimum-wage; accessed 27 July 2011.
5. *Bangkok Post*, 15 July 2011.
6. *Bangkok Post*, 21 July 2011.
7. www.humanrights.asia/news/forwarded-news/AHRC-FST-048-2011.
8. 'Hopes for Peace in Thai–Cambodia Border', 30 July 2011, www.asia-calling.org/en/news/thailand/2137-hopes-for-peace-in-thai-cambodia-border.
9. Turnell et al. 2010.
10. See Appendix 2 for the kyat–dollar exchange rate 1997–2005.
11. *Bangkok Post*, 24 July 2011.
12. *Bangkok Post*, 13 November 2011.

13. *Bangkok Post*, 24 July 2011.
14. The Reith Lectures are a series of annual radio lectures on significant contemporary issues delivered by leading figures of the day, commissioned by the BBC, and broadcast on BBC Radio 4 and the BBC World Service. They are available on www.bbc.co.uk/programmes/b00729d9.
15. Lee 1998: 10-11.

References

ACMECS (2004). 'Ayeyawady-Chao Phraya-Mekong Economic Cooperation Strategy'. ACMECS Ministerial Retreat, Krabi, Thailand, 2 November, www.acmecs.org/index.php.

Amnesty International (2005). 'Thailand: The Plight of Burmese Migrant Workers'. *AI Index.* New York: Amnesty International.

Archavanitkul, K. (2002). *Research Direction and Knowledge about Migrants* (Thai). Institute for Population and Social Research, Mahidol University, Thailand.

Arnold, D. (2004). *The Situation of Burmese Migrant Workers in Mae Sot, Thailand.* Working Papers Series, No. 71. City University of Hong Kong.

Arnold, D. (2006). 'Capital Expansion and Migrant Workers: Flexible Labour in the Thai-Burma Border Economy'. M.A. dissertation, Faculty of Graduate Studies, Mahidol University, Thailand.

Arnold, D., and K. Hewison (2005). 'Exploitation in Global Supply Chains: Burmese Migrant Workers in Mae Sot, Thailand'. *Journal of Contemporary Asia* 35(3).

Arnold, D., and J. Pickles (2011). 'Global Work, Surplus Labour, and the Precarious Economies of the Border'. *Antipode* 43(5).

Asian Human Rights Commission (2005). *Update on Urgent Appeal.* Asian Human Rights Commission, Hong Kong, 16 September.

Asian Research Center for Migration (ARCM), Institute for Population and Social Research (IPSR), and Thailand Development Research Institute Foundation (TDRI) (2004). *Thailand: Improving the Management of Foreign Workers: Case Studies on Five Industrial Sectors'.* Prepared for the International Organization for Migration and International Labour Organization (ILO), International Organization for Migration, Mission with Regional Functions, Bangkok.

Aung, K., and S.L. Aung (2009). *Critical Times: Migrants and the Economy in Chiang Mai and Mae Sot*. Chiang Mai: MAP Foundation.

Barrientos, A. (2007). 'Does Vulnerability Create Poverty Traps?', Working Paper No. 76, Chronic Poverty Research Centre, University of Manchester.

Behrman, J.R., A.B. Deolalikar et al. (2001). 'The Effects of the Thai Economic Crisis and of Thai Labour Market Policies on Labour Market Outcomes: Executive Summary'. *TDRI Quarterly Review* 16(3): 3–9.

Caouette, T.M. (2001). *Small Dreams Beyond Reach: The Lives of Migrant Children and Youth Along the Borders of China, Myanmar and Thailand*, London: Save the Children UK.

Caouette, T.M., et al. (2006). *Labour Migration in the Greater Mekong Subregion*. Bangkok: Rockefeller Foundation.

Chalamwong, Y., and S. Amornthum (2002). *Thailand: Improving Migration Policy Management with Special Focus on Irregular Labour Migration – Analysis of Thai Labour Market*. Bangkok: Thailand Development Research Institute Foundation.

Charoenlert, V., and B. Thanachaisettavuth (1997). *Industrial Development Policy and Migrant Employment*. Institute for Population and Social Research, Mahidol University, Thailand.

Charoenlert, V., and B. Thanachaisettavuth (eds) (2001). *Wikrit sethakid sangkhom kpa anakot reng gann thai* [Socio-economic Crisis and the Future of Thai labour]. *2540 chut plien prathet thai* (1997 Turning point of Thailand), Political Economy Center.

Chulalongkorn University (2003). *Migrant Workers from Burma and Thailand: Policy Review and Protection Mechanisms, Commemorating 10 years of Policy Governing Migrant Workers from Burma*. Proceedings of a seminar on Reviewing Policies and Creating Mechanisms to Protect Migrant Workers. Chulalongkorn University, Thailand.

Davin, D. (1998). 'Gender and Migration in China'. In *Village Inc.: Chinese Rural Society in the 1990s*, ed. F. Christiansen and Z. Junzuo. London: Curzon.

Ekachai, S (2007). 'A Place To Learn: An Oasis for Migrant Children Thirsty for Education', *Stateless Person*, Human Rights Sub-Committee on Ethnic Minorities, Stateless, Migrant Workers and Displaced Persons, Lawyers Council of Thailand.

Elson, D., and R. Pearson (1981). '"Nimble Fingers Make Cheap Workers": An Analysis of Women's Employment in Third World Export Manufacturing'. *Feminist Review* 7: 87–107.

ESCAP (Economic and Social Commission for Asia and the Pacific) (2003). *Social Safety Nets for Women*. Studies on Gender and Development. New York: United Nations.

Fink, C. (2009). *Living Silence: Burma under Military Rule*. London and New York: Zed Books.

Friedrich-Ebert-Stiftung and Women Workers' Unity Group (n.d.). *For Thailand's Woman Workers: Twelve Years of Struggle*, Bangkok, http://library.fes.de/pdf-files/bueros/thailand/50112.pdf.

Fröbel,F., J. Heinrichs and O. Kreye. (1980) *The New International Division of Labour*. Cambridge: Cambridge University Press.

FTUB (Federation of Trade Unions - Burma) (2004). *Brief Report on Child Migrant Workers from Burma in Thailand, Case study — Mae Sot*.

FTUB Migrants Section and P.S. Robertson Jr (2006) 'The Mekong Challenge - Working Day and Night: The Plight of Migrant Child Workers in Mae Sot, Thailand'. *Mekong Sub-Regional Project to Combat Trafficking in Children and Women*. International Programme on the Elimination of Child Labour, International Labour Organization, Bangkok.

Gillogly, K. (2004). 'Developing the "Hill Tribes" of Northern Thailand'. In *Civilizing the Margins: Southeast Asian Government Policies for the Development of Minorities*, ed. C.R. Duncan. Ithaca NY: Cornell University Press.

Harada, Y., and I. Yasuhisa (1998). *Thai Keizai Nyumon* [Japanese] [Introduction to the Thai Economy]. Tokyo: Nihon Hyouron-sha.

Hayami, Y. (2004). *Between Hills and Plains: Power and Practice in Socioreligious Dynamics Among Karen*. Kyoto Area Studies on Asia. Kyoto: Kyoto University Press and Trans Pacific Press.

Hicken, A. (ed.) (2008). *The Politics of Economic Recovery in Thailand and the Philippines. Crisis as Catalyst: Asia's Dynamic Political Economy*. Ithaca NY: Cornell University Press.

Hochschild, A. (2000). 'Global Care Chains and Emotional Surplus Value'. In *On the Edge: Living with Global Capitalism*, ed. W. Hutton and A. Giddens. London: Jonathan Cape.

Huguet, J.W. (2007). 'Thailand'sPolicy Approach to Irregular Migration'. In *The Contribution of Migrant Workers to Thailand: Towards Policy Development*, ed. P. Martin. Bangkok: International Labour Office.

Huguet, J.W., and S. Punpuing (2005). *International Migration in Thailand*. Bangkok: International Organization for Migration.

Human Rights Watch. (2010). *From the Tiger to the Crocodile: Abuse of Migrant Workers in Thailand*. New York.

Hveem, P., and E.B. Than Doke (2004). *Hidden Exploitation: Burmese Migrants in Thai Garment Factories — Hidden Sub-contracting by Tommy Hilfiger Corporation and Other Brands, Mae Sot, Thailand*. Oslo: Norwegian Church Aid.

ILO (International Labour Organization) (2002). *Women and Men in the Informal Economy: A Statistical Picture*. Geneva.

ILO (International Labour Organization), Regional Office for Asia and the Pacific. (2007). *Labour and Social Trends in ASEAN 2007: Integration, Challenges and Opportunities*. Bangkok.

IOM (International Organization for Migration) (2005). *COA Thailand Burmese Cultural Profile: A Tool for Settlement Workers*. Bangkok.

Institute of Asian Studies, Chulalongkorn University, Thailand Development Research Institute (TDRI), The Institute for Population and Social Research (IPSR) and Mahidol University (2003). *Research Project: Demand of Migrant Worker in Thailand 2003–2005*. Submitted to the National Security Council, Prime Minister's Office, October.

Joekes, S. (1987). *Women in the World Economy.* New York: Oxford University Press.

Kojima, Y. (2007). *Women in the Trafficking–Migration Continuum:From the Perspective of Human Rights and Social Justice.* Maastricht: Shaker Publishing.

Kusakabe, K. (2006). *Reconciling Work and Family: Issues and Policies in Thailand.* Conditions of Work and Employment Series, No. 14. Conditions of Work and Employment Programme. Geneva: International Labour Organization.

Kusakabe, K., and R. Pearson (2010). 'Transborder Migration, Social Reproduction and Economic Development: A Case Study of Burmese Women Workers in Thailand'. *International Migration* 48(6): 13-43.

Lee, C.K. (1998). *Gender and the South Asian Miracle: Two Worlds of Factory Women.* Berkeley: University of California Press.

Ling, D. (2007). 'Burmese Migrant Workers' Access to Health Care Services in Thailand'. M.Sc. thesis. Asian Institute of Technology, Bangkok.

Luthichai, S. (2003). 'The Views of Employers towards Foreign Labour in Samut Sakorn Province' [Thai]. Master's thesis. Mahidol University, Thailand.

MAP Foundation (n.d.). '*The Regulation of Migrant Workers following the MOUs*', www.mapfoundationcm.org/Eng/MOUupdate.html.

Martin, P. (2007). *The Contribution of Migrant Workers to Thailand: Towards Policy Development.* Bangkok: International Labour Office.

Martin, P., et al. (2004). *Thailand: Improving the Management of Foreign Workers.* Bangkok: Asian Research Center for Migration.

McCargo, D.J. (2008). *Tearing apart the Land: Islam and Legitimacy in Southern Thailand.* Ithaca NY: Cornell University Press.

McCarthy, S. (2010). 'Legitimacy under Military Rule: Burma'. *Politics & Policy* 38(3): 545-69.

Mekong Migration Network and Asian Migration Centre (2008). *Migration in the Greater Mekong Subregion Resource Book: In-depth Study – Arrest, Detention and Deportation.* Hong Kong: Clear Cut Publishing.

Ministry of Labour (2005). *Year Book of Labour Protection and Welfare Statistics, 2004.* Bangkok.

Naing, S. Y. (2008). 'Economic Slowdown Hits Burmese Migrant Workers in Thailand'. *Irrawady News*, 28 November 2008.

Ngai, Pun (2005). *Made in China: Women Factory Workers in a Global Workplace.* Durham NC: Duke University Press.

Nwe, T.T. (2003). 'Gendered Spaces: Women in Burmese Society'. *Transformations* 6, February.

ODI (Overseas Development Institute) (2011). *Mapping Progress: Evidence for a New Development Outlook.* London.

Office of the National Economic and Social Development Board (2003). 'Thai Border Economic Cooperation'. PowerPoint presentation.

Ogena, N., et al. (1997). *Globalization with Equity: Policies for Growth in Thailand*, Nakhon Pathom Institute for Population and Social Research, Mahidol University, Thailand.

Pearson, E., et al. (2006). 'Mekong Challenge – Underpaid, Overworked and Overlooked: The Realities of Young Migrant Workers in Thailand', *Mekong Sub-regional Project to Combat Trafficking in Children and Women*. Bangkok: International Labour Office.

Pearson, R. (1995). 'Gender Perspectives on Health and Safety in Information Processing: Learning from International Experience'. In *Women Encounter Technology: Changing Patterns of Employment in the Third World*, ed. W. Mitter and S. Rowbotham. London: Routledge.

Pearson, R., and K. Kusakabe (2012) 'Who Cares? Gender, Reproduction and Care Chains of Burmese Migrant Factory Workers in Thailand'. *Feminist Economics*, Special Issue on Gender and Migration, 19(2), April.

Pearson, R., and G. Seyfang (2001). 'New Hope or False Dawn? Voluntary Codes of Conduct, Labour Regulation and Social Policy in a Globalising World'. *Global Social Policy* 1(1): 49–78.

Pearson, R., and G. Seyfang (2002). "I'll tell you what I want...." Women Workers and Codes of Conduct'. In *Corporate Responsibility and Labour Rights: Codes of Conduct in the Global Economy*, ed. R. Jenkins, R. Person and G. Seyfang. London: Earthscan.

Phillips, A., and B. Taylor (1980). 'Sex and Skills: Notes towards a Feminist Economics'. *Feminist Review* 6: 79–88.

Phongpaichit, P., and C. Baker (1998). *Thailand's Boom and Bust*. Chiang Mai: Silkworm Books.

Phongpaichit, P., and C. Baker (2000). *Thailand's Crisis*. Chiang Mai: Silkworm Books.

Pollock, J. (2006). *Cross-border Migration: Burma–Thailand*. Paper presented at Asian Consultation on Gender, Migration and Citizenship, ARI-NUS and IDRC, Singapore.

Pollock, J., and S.L. Aung (2010). 'Critical Times: Gendered Implications of the Economic Crisis for Migrant Workers from Burma/Myanmar in Thailand'. *Gender and Development* 18(2): 213–27.

Pornthipsathern, S. (2003). 'Social Problems Caused by Employment of Foreign Workers at See-Moom Muang Market in Pathumthani Province' (Thai). Master's thesis. Chulalongkorn University, Thailand.

Punpuing, S., et al. (2006). *The Mekong Challenge: Underpaid, Overworked and Overlooked – The Realities of Young Migrant Workers in Thailand*, Vol. 2. International Programme on the Elimination of Child Labour. Bangkok: International Labour Organization.

Razavi, S. (1999). 'Export-Oriented Employment, Poverty and Gender: Contested Accounts'. *Development and Change* 30: 653–83.

Sciortino, R., and S. Punpuing (2009). *International Migration in Thailand*. Bangkok: International Organization for Migration.

Seekins, D.M. (2009). 'Myanmar 2008: Hardship, Compounded'. *Asian Survey* 49(1): 166–73.

Shafaeddin, S.M. (2004). 'Is China's Accession to WTO Threatening Exports of Developing Countries?' *China Economic Review* 15(2): 109–44.

Skeldon, R. (1999). 'Migration in Asia after the Economic Crisis: Patterns and Issues'. *Asia–Pacific Population Journal* 14(3): 3–24.

Somers, M.R. (1994). 'The Narrative Construction of Identity: A Relational and Network Approach'. *Theory and Society* 23: 605–49.

Stratton, A. (2008) 'Burma Referendum Begins While Aid Trickles In'. *Guardian*, 10 May 2008.

Suehiro, A. (2000). *Catch Up Gata Kougyou-ron* [Catching up Industrialization], Tokyo: Nagoya University Press.

TDRI (Thailand Development Research Institute) (2002). *Thailand Economic Information Kit*, www.info.tdri.or/th; accessed March 2006.

Thammasak, A. (1998) *Workers' Situation and Needs for Remuneration: A Comparative Study between Thai and Foreign Workers in Samutprakan Province* (in Thai), M.A. dissertation, Mahidol University, Thailand.

Theobald, S. (2001) 'Working for Global Factories: Thai Women in Electronics Export Companies in the Northern Regional Industrial Estate', in *Women and Work in Globalizing Asia*, ed. D.S. Gills and N. Piper. London: Routledge.

Traitongyoo, K. (2008). 'The Management of Irregular Migration in Thailand: Thainess, Identity and Citizenship'. Ph.D. thesis, School of Politics and International Studies, University of Leeds.

Tsuneishi, T. (2005). *The Regional Development Policy of Thailand and Its Economic Cooperation with Neighbouring Countries*. Institute of Development Economics, Japan External Trade Organization, Tokyo.

Turnell, S., A. Vicary and W. Bradford (2010). 'Migrant Worker Remittances and Burma: An Economic Analysis of Survey Results'. *Burma Economic Watch*, Macquarie University, Sydney.

UN-INSTRAW (2007). *The Feminization of International Labour Migration*. New York: United Nations International Research and Training Institute for the Advancement of Women.

UNCHR (United Nations High Commissioner for Refugees) (2011). *Global Appeal 2011 Update: Restoring Hope Rebuilding Lives: Thailand*. Geneva.

Unger, D. (1998). *Building Social Capital in Thailand: Fibres, Finance and Infrastructure*. Cambridge: Cambridge University Press.

Wai, M. (2004). *A Memoir of Burmese Workers: From Slave Labour to Illegal Migrant Workers*. Bangkok: Thai Action Committee for Democracy in Burma (TACDB).

Wansiripaisan, P. (2002). *Foreign Labour Employment: Social Impact and the Role of Civil Society*. Bangkok: National Research Council of Thailand.

World Vision and Asian Research Center for Migration (2003). *Research Report on Migration and Deception of Migrant Workers in Thailand*. Chulalongkorn University, Thailand.

Yeates, N. (2009). *Globalizing Care Economies and Migrant workers: Explorations in Global Care Chain*. Basingstoke: Palgrave Macmillan.

Yimprasert, J., and P. Hveem (2005). *The Race to the Bottom: Exploitation of Workers in the Global Garment Industry*. Oslo: Norwegian Church Aid.

Index

Mon ethnic group, 3, 56, 109, 123, 150, 157
Morocco, 9
motorcycles, ban on migrant use, 27
MOU (Memorandum of Understanding), on registration of migrant labour, 14, 35, 38, 42, 90, 174
Mukdahan province, 26
Muslims, Burmese, 5
Myitsone dam, Burma suspended, 171

Nandar Cho, 64
Nandar Choyangon, garment factories, 68
National League for Democracy, Burma, 170
national security rhetoric, Thailand, 42, 151
nationality verification process, 38, 50, 79-81, 168
NGOs (non-governmental organisations), 84, 88; clinics, 128; education, 129; welfare, 140
Nicaragua, 9
Nike, 25
NLD Party, Burma, 20
non-Thai ethnicities, Thai hostility to, 16
North America, border development model, 27; Burmese diaspora, 2

opportunities, Burma lack, 66; thought of, 56
original documents, employer held, 89
outsourcing, international, 11
overtime, 85

Pa-O, ethnic group, 56
parents: duty to sense, 58-9, 123, 139; education focus, 67; grandchild care, 115-17; migrant daughters ambivalence, 68-9; return pressure, 161; Thailand visits, 69; women's obligations to, 71-2

parliamentary rule, 1997 restoration, 38
passport system, costs of, 41
Pathaumthani province, Thailand, 5
Pattanarak Foundation, 141
Pearson, Elaine, 170
Pheu Thai Party (ex-Thai Rak Thai), 166-9
Phuket province, migrant worker restrictions, 38
piece rates, childcare implications, 122
police, Thailand: powers, 37; raids on migrants, 66, 79, 98, 100
Pollock, Jackie, 167
poverty reduction, Thailand, 44
pregnancy, migrant women, 107-8: continuation decision, 112; illegal termination, 127; terminations, 111
Private Insurance Scheme for Migrant Workers, 169
'Protect Thai jobs', rhetoric, 33
Punpuing, S., 83, 89

Rakhaing, ethnic group, 56, State, 77
Ranong, migrant workers, 47
rape, Burmese strategic, 170
Rayong province, migrant workers curfew, 38
Red shirts, Thailand, 166
refugees, Burmese, 2
registration system/schemes (migrants in Thailand), 7, 14, 33, 35, 40, 44, 55, 167; avoidance motives, 81; Bangkok, 79; costs of, 94, 150; different levels, 79; employer favoured, 41; employers' avoidance, 50, 173; MOU system, 38, 42, 90, 174; 1996 scheme, 36; obstacles, 39; procedures, 101; public attitudes, 43; recruitment difficulties, 84; 2011 scheme, 168
'regulating the irregular', system of, 33

114; Thai Rak Thai Party, 24;
vigilantes, 44, 145, 154; wage
rises, 44; workers, *see above*;
xenophobia increase, 151
Thaksin Shinawatra, 20, 24, 30, 38,
166
'3D' jobs, 13, 36, 43, 47, 134
Three Pagodas Pass (*Payathonzu*),
Kanchanaburi province, 5-6, 19,
28, 48, 57-8, 63, 67, 75, 78-9, 84,
86, 88, 92, 94-5, 98-9, 100, 102,
104-5, 108-10, 112, 114, 121, 123,
125-7, 134, 136, 158-9, 162, 165;
Bangkok subcontracted factories,
54; childcare, 118; daily cross-
border workers, 55; Pattanarak
Foundation, 141; piece-rate
factories, 53
tight production schedules, 19
Tin Moe Aung, 64
Tin Nwe Soe, 59, 91, 142-5
Tommy Hilfiger, 51
Top Form International, 51
trade unions, 23, 43, 84, 88
trafficking, 63
Turnell, Sean, 169

Ubon Ratchathani province, 26
UN (United Nations) anti-malaria
nets production, 54; Commission
of Trade and Development, 167;
Convention on Transnational
Organized Crime, 34; High
Commission on Refugees, 176;
1951 Convention on Refugees, 172
unemployment, garment sector, 135
unionisation, Thai rate of, 23
'unregistered' migrants, 1; employer
bound, 42; police raids on, 50;
threats to, 85
USA (United States of America), 48;
Burma investment ban, 32;
Mexico border, 10

Vejajiva, Abhisit, 20, 151
Vietnam, 4, 9, 24, 26, 133
Vitanakorn, Vallop, 30

wages: different minimum levels,
94; minimum, 29, 53, 167; non-
payment of, 93, 155; non-payment
disputes, 148-9; Thai-Burma
difference, 4; underpayment, 94;
unpaid overtime dispute, 141-2;
withheld, 88
Wandee Seebua-iam, 168
Wide Horizon programme, 'World
Education', 129
women: Burmese extended family,
66; childcare, *see above*; 'docile'
worker label, 147; global crisis
shock absorbers, 139; multiple
roles, 72-3; preferred labour
force, 9; registration
disincentives, 101; remittances
behaviour, 71; South China
workers, 76; workers' life cycle,
107; young in Thai factories, 7,
47
work permits, fees for, 36, 40, 94
Workers' Compensation Fund,
169
working hours, length of, 85-6,
123
Workmen's Compensation Fund,
Thailand, 23
World Bank, 22, 133
World Vision, 140

Yangon, Burma, 28, 50, 64, 71, 87,
97, 103-4, 125, 142; garment
factories, 57-9, 61, 64-5, 67-8, 86,
104
Yaung Chi Oo Workers' Association,
140-41
Yinluck Shinawatra, 20, 166
Yunnan, 82

About Zed Books

Zed Books is a critical and dynamic publisher, committed to increasing awareness of important international issues and to promoting diversity, alternative voices and progressive social change. We publish on politics, development, gender, the environment and economics for a global audience of students, academics, activist and general readers. Run as a co-operative, we aim to operate in an ethical and environmentally sustainable way.

Find out more at
www.zedbooks.co.uk

For up-to-date news, articles, reviews
and events information visit
http://zed-books.blogspot.com

To subscribe to the monthly Zed Books e-newsletter
send an email headed 'subscribe' to marketing@zedbooks.net

We can also be found on Facebook, ZNet,
Twitter and Library Thing.